THIS BOOK BELONGS TO

NAME:
AGE:
ADDRESS:

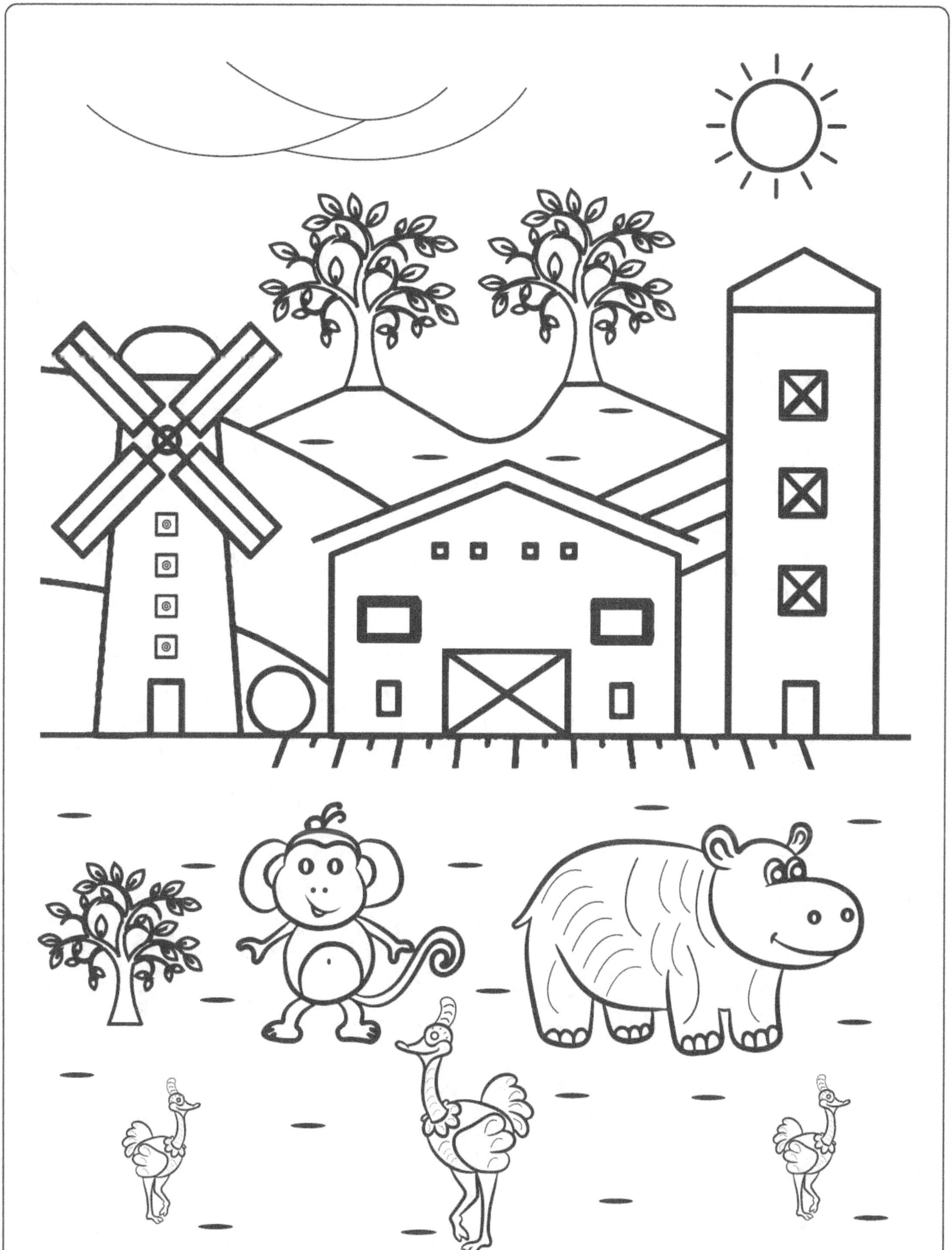

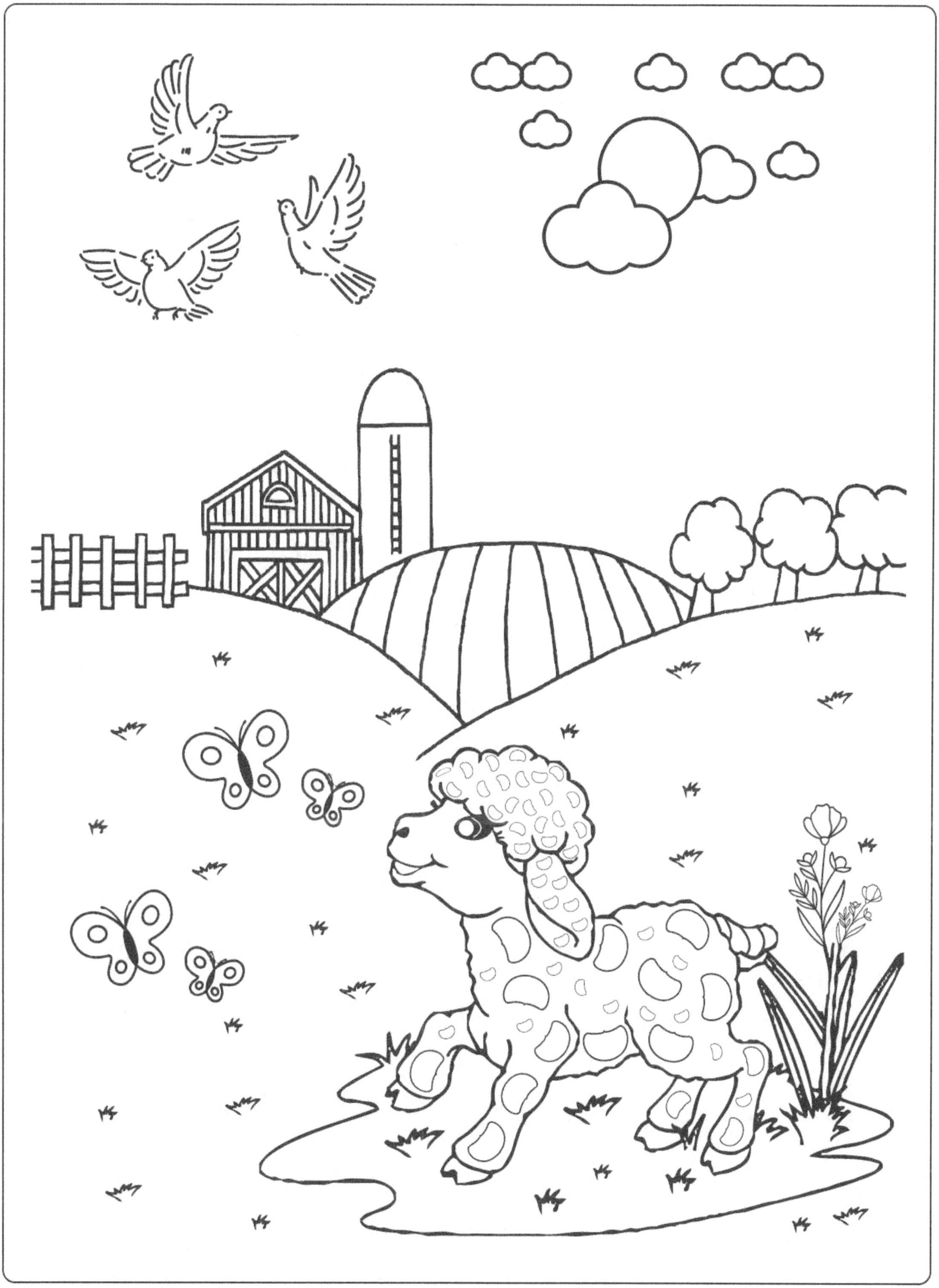

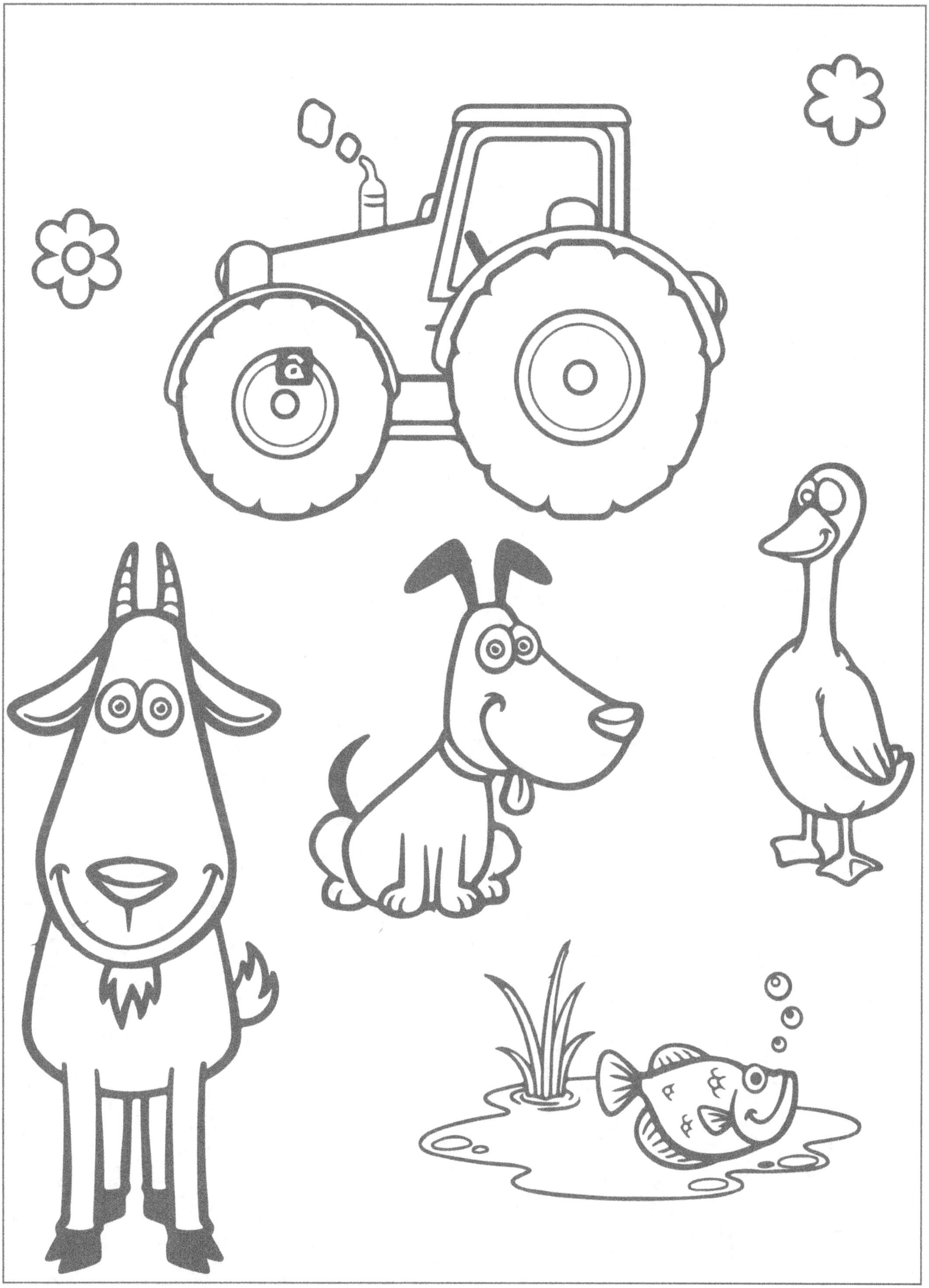

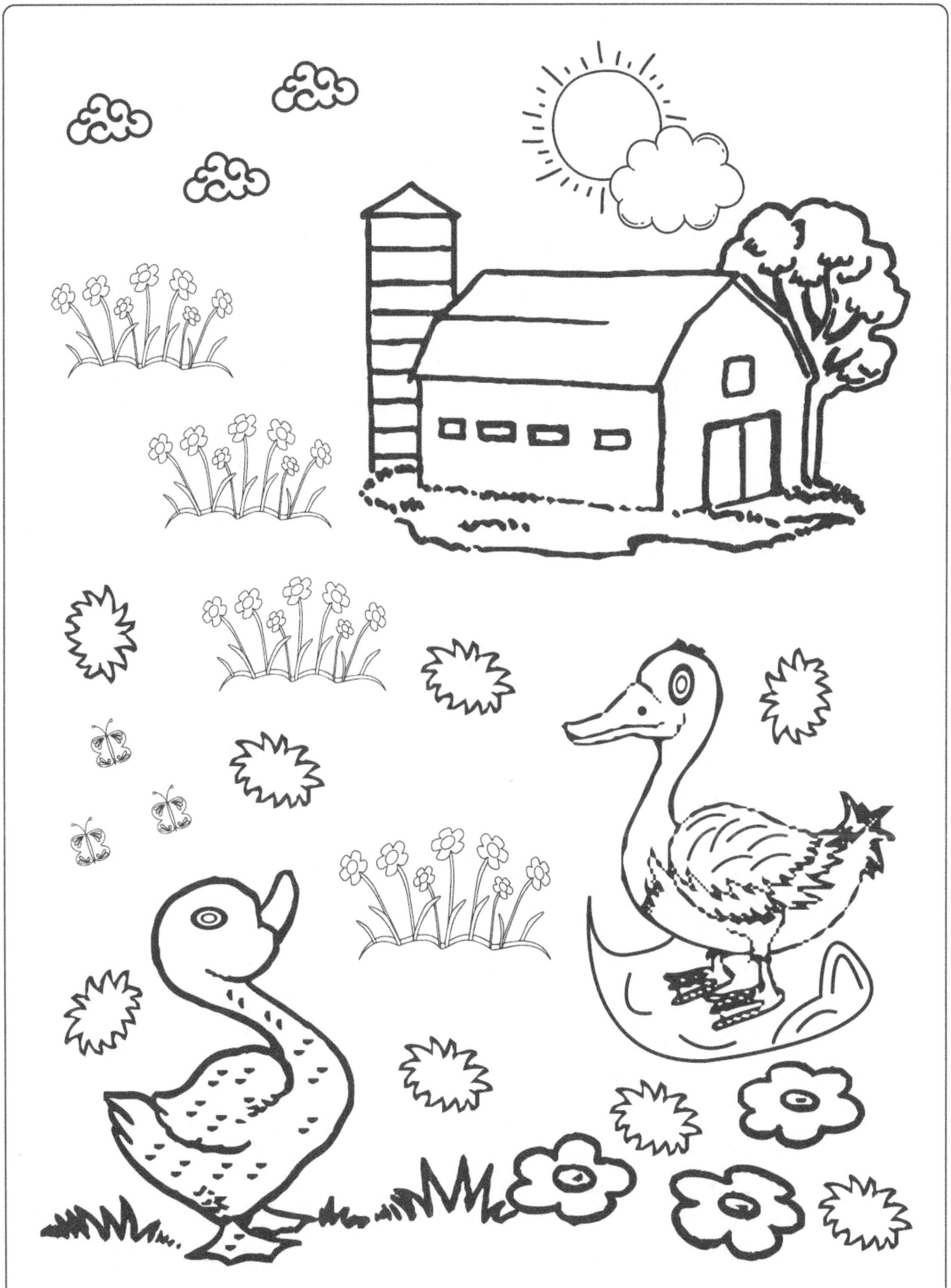

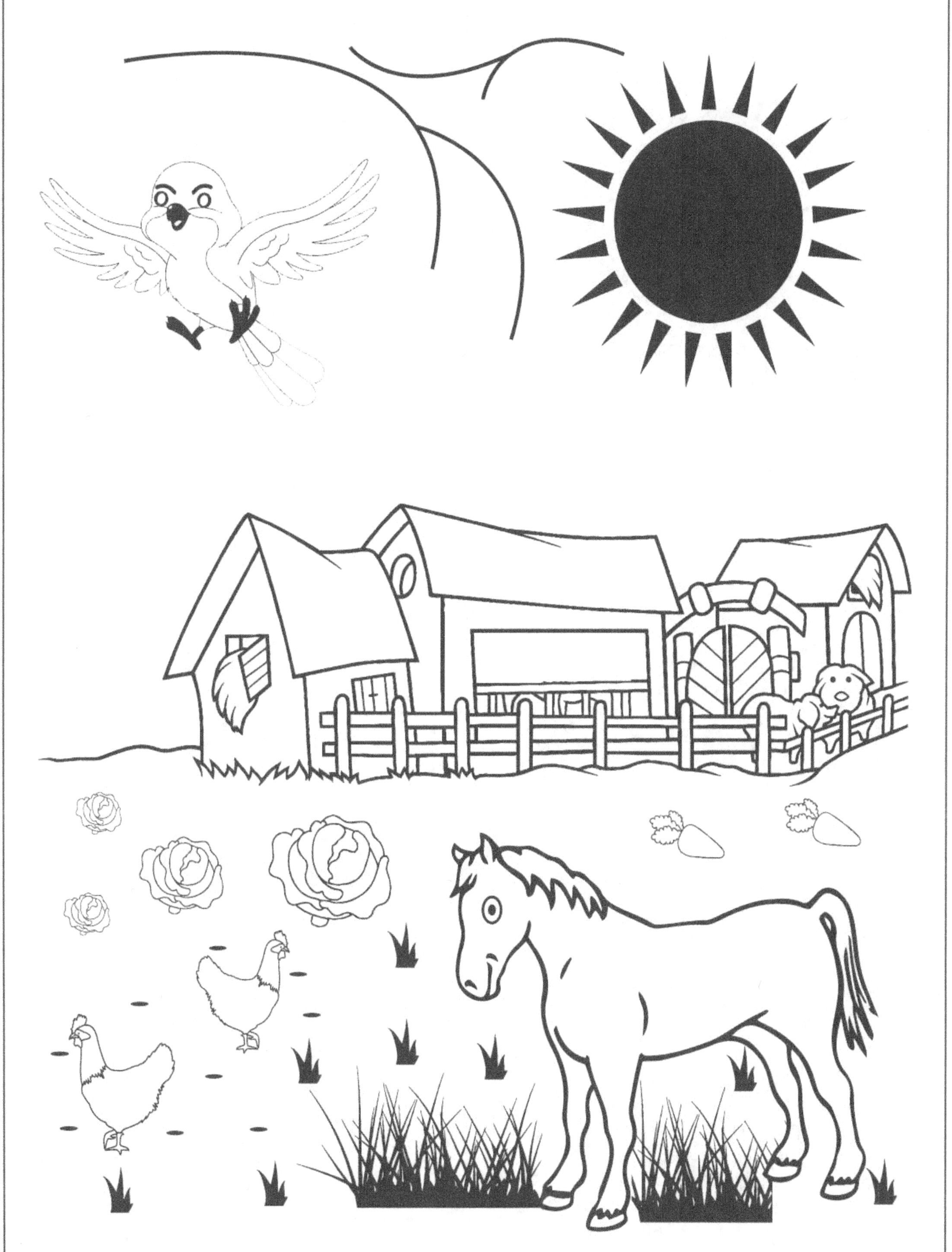

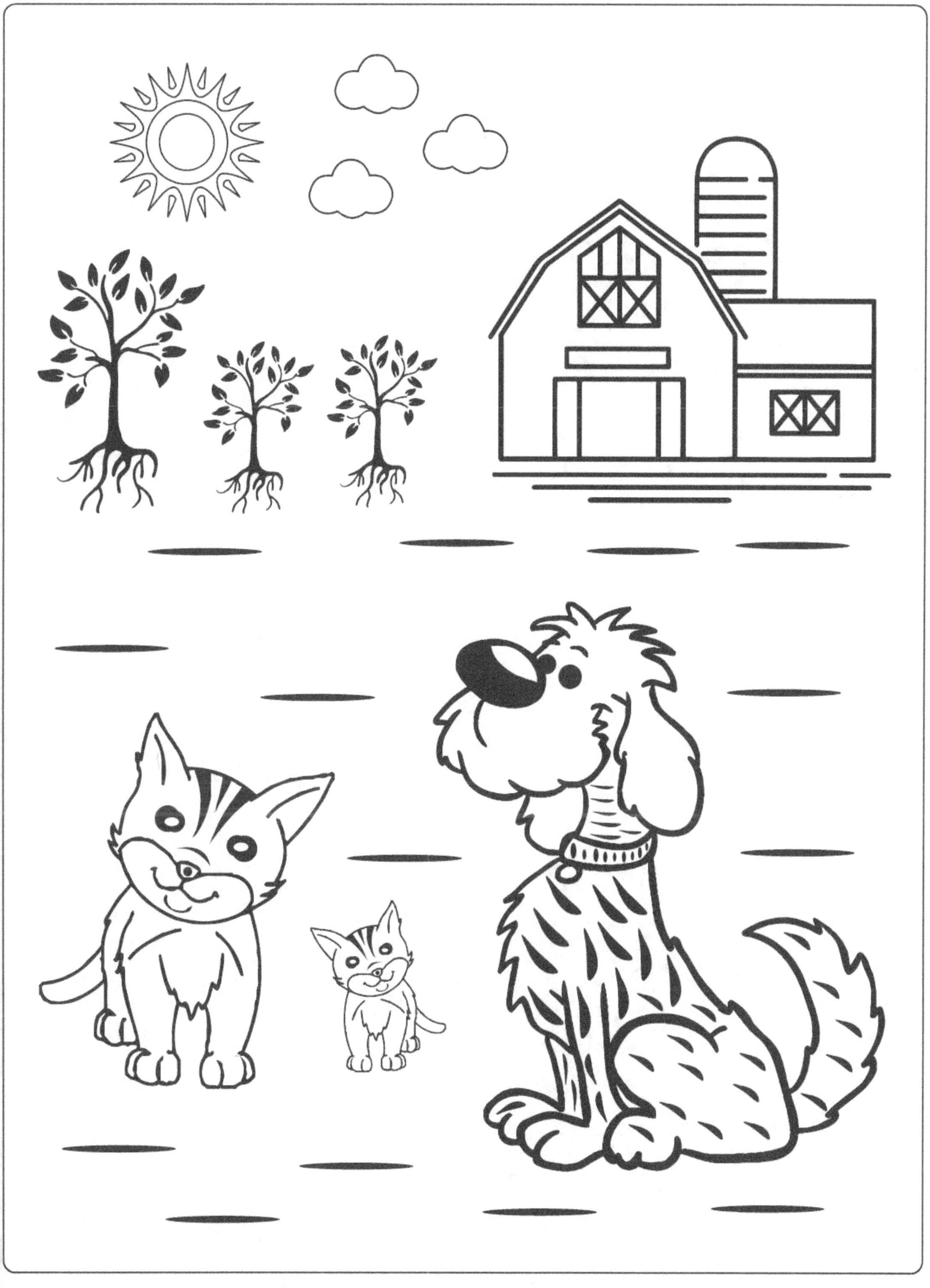

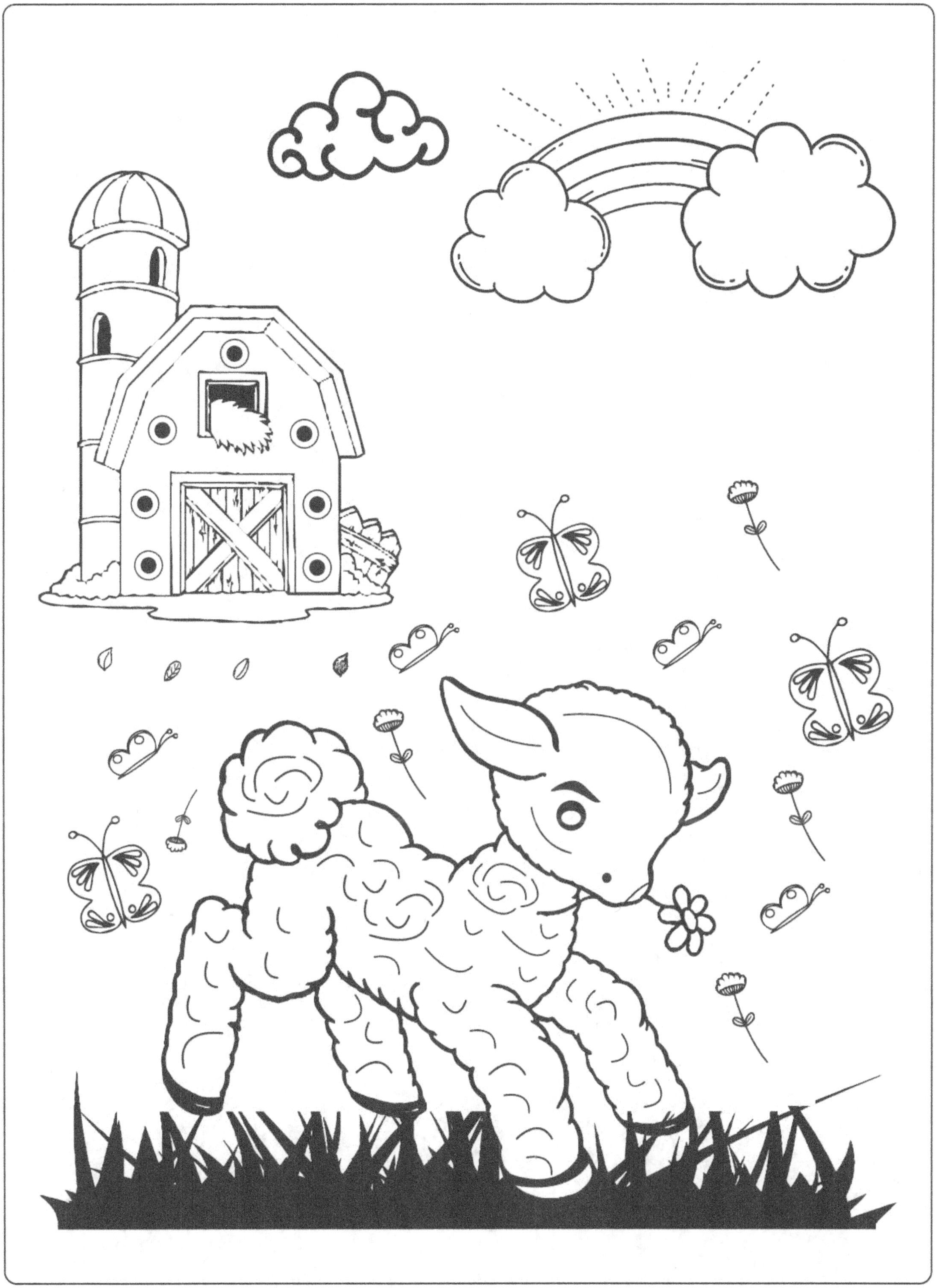

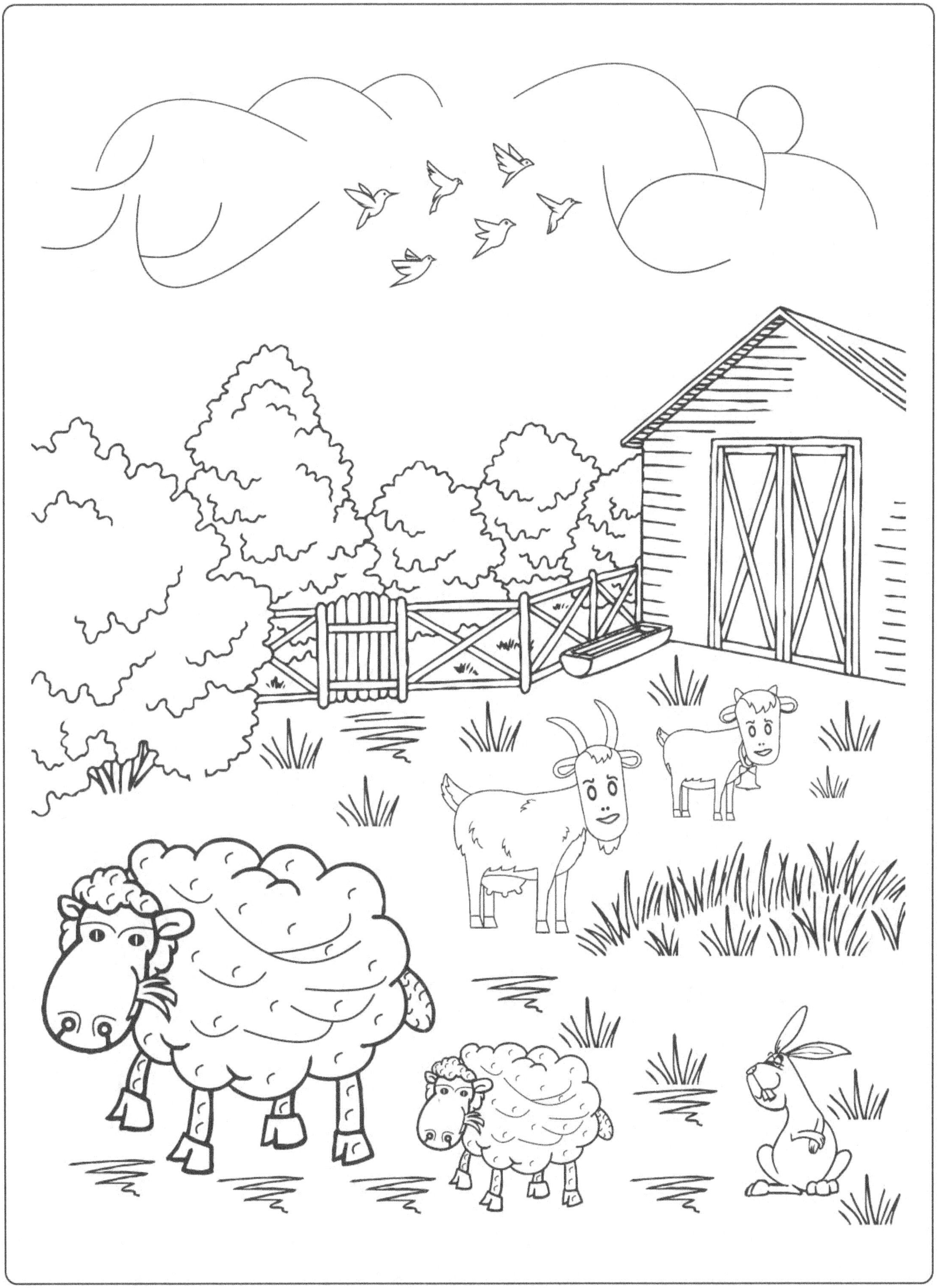

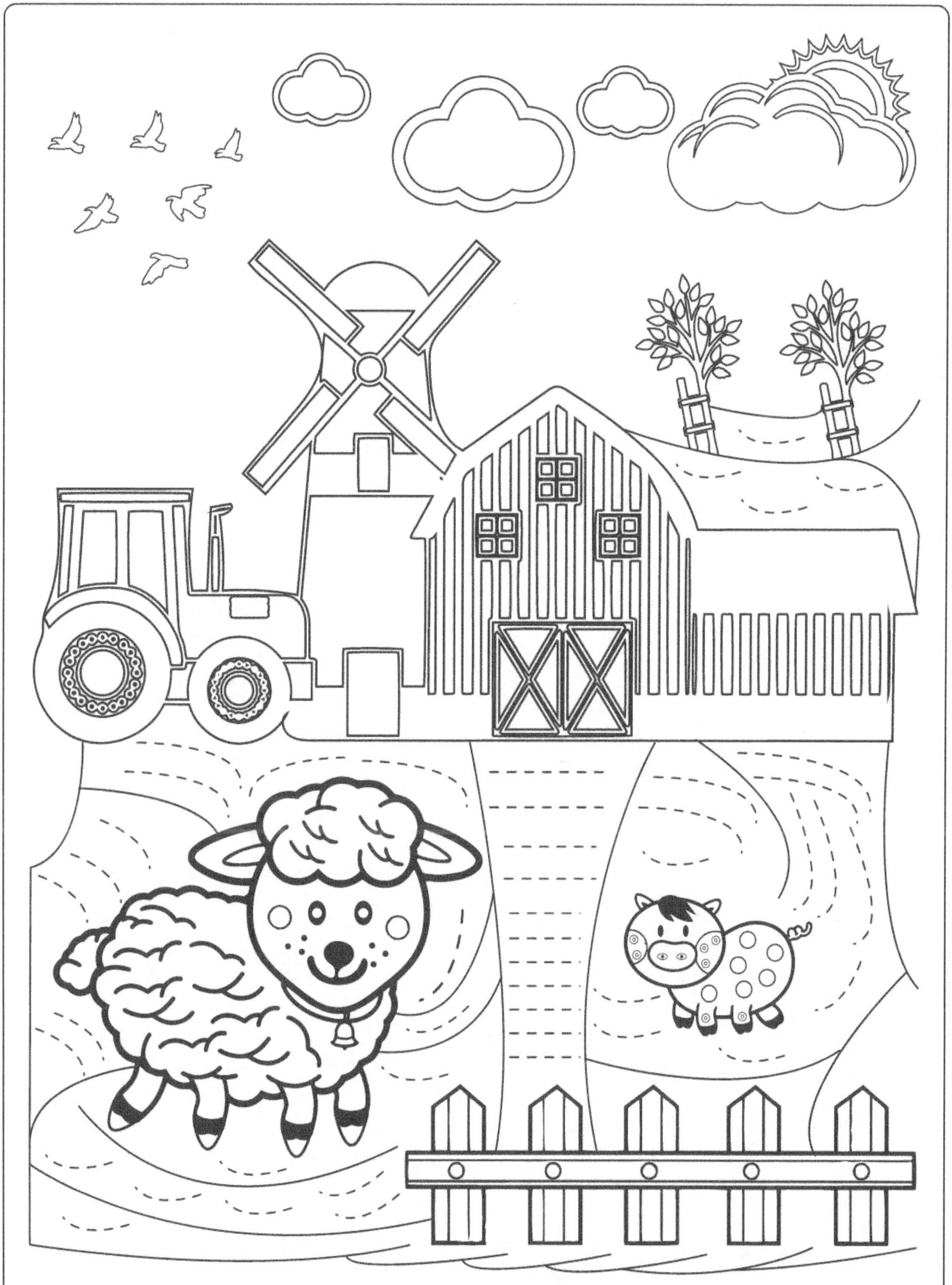

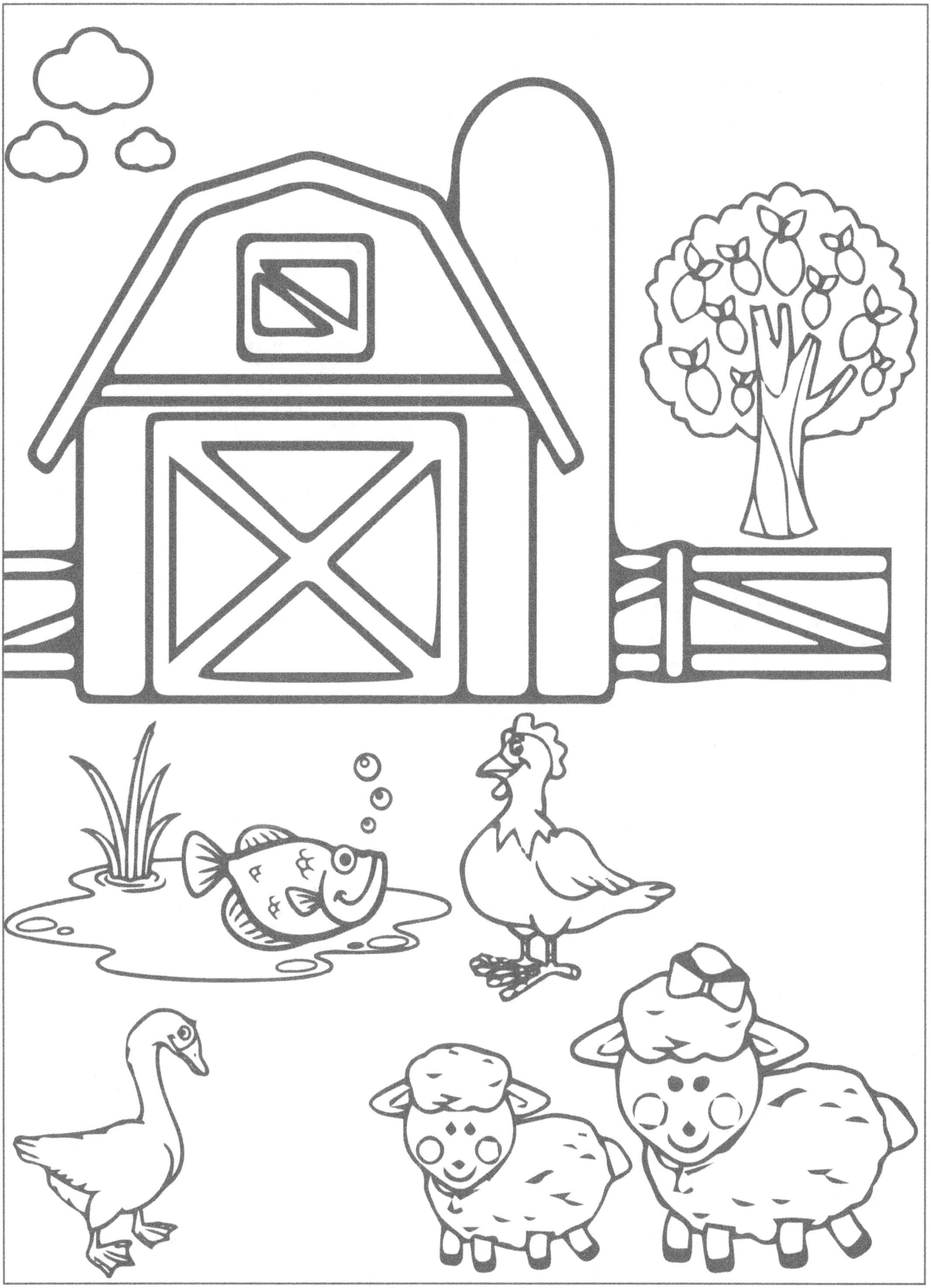

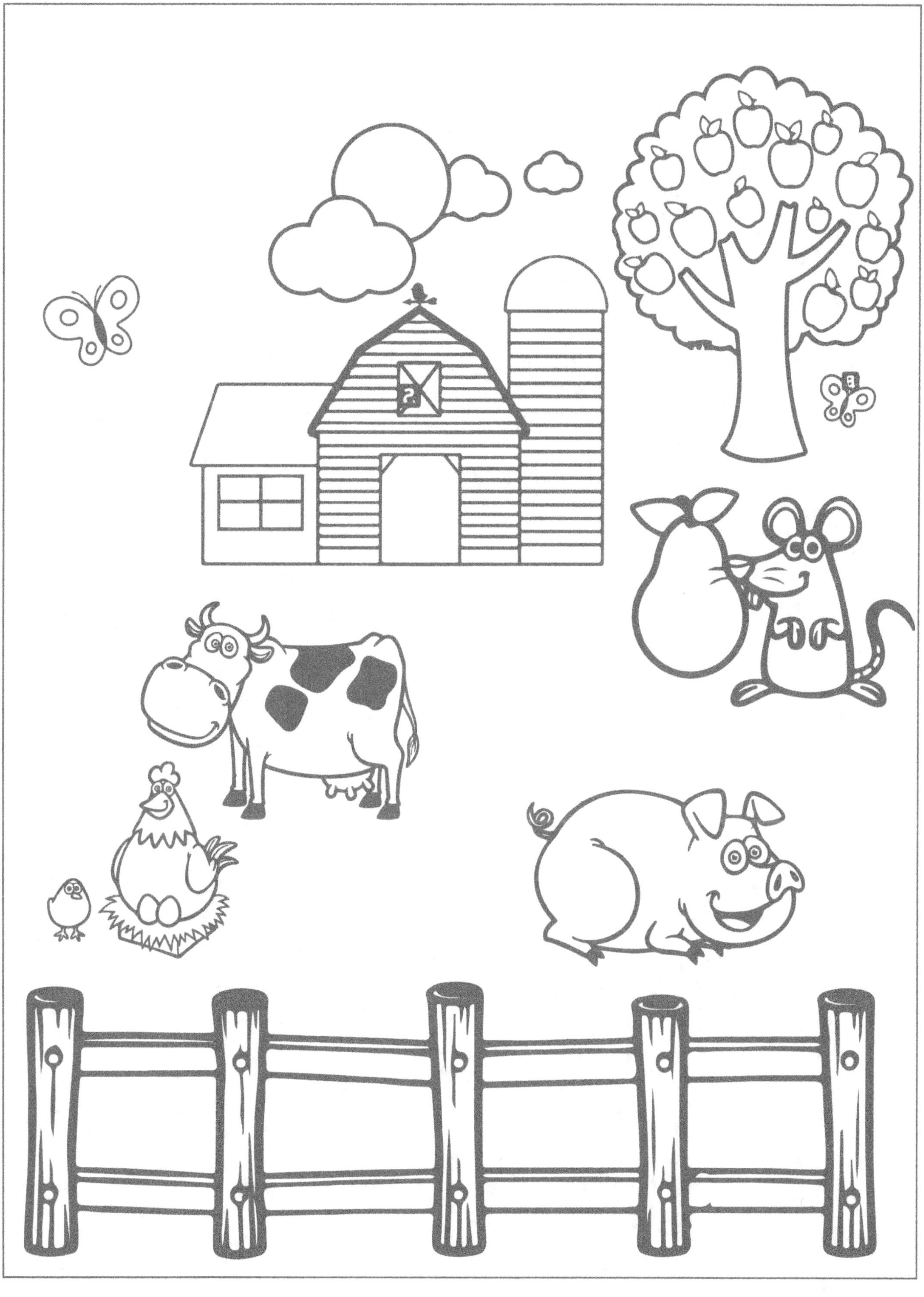

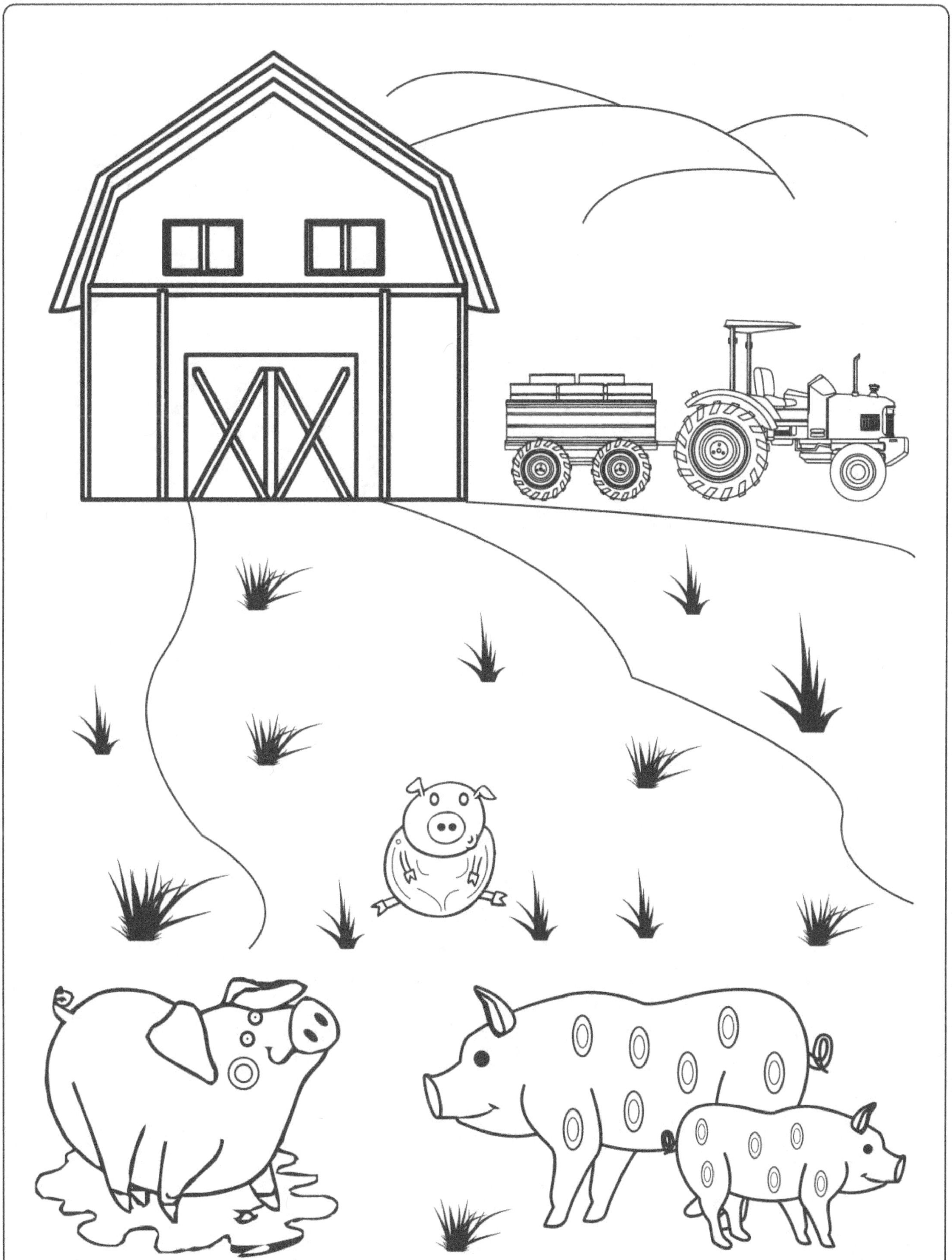

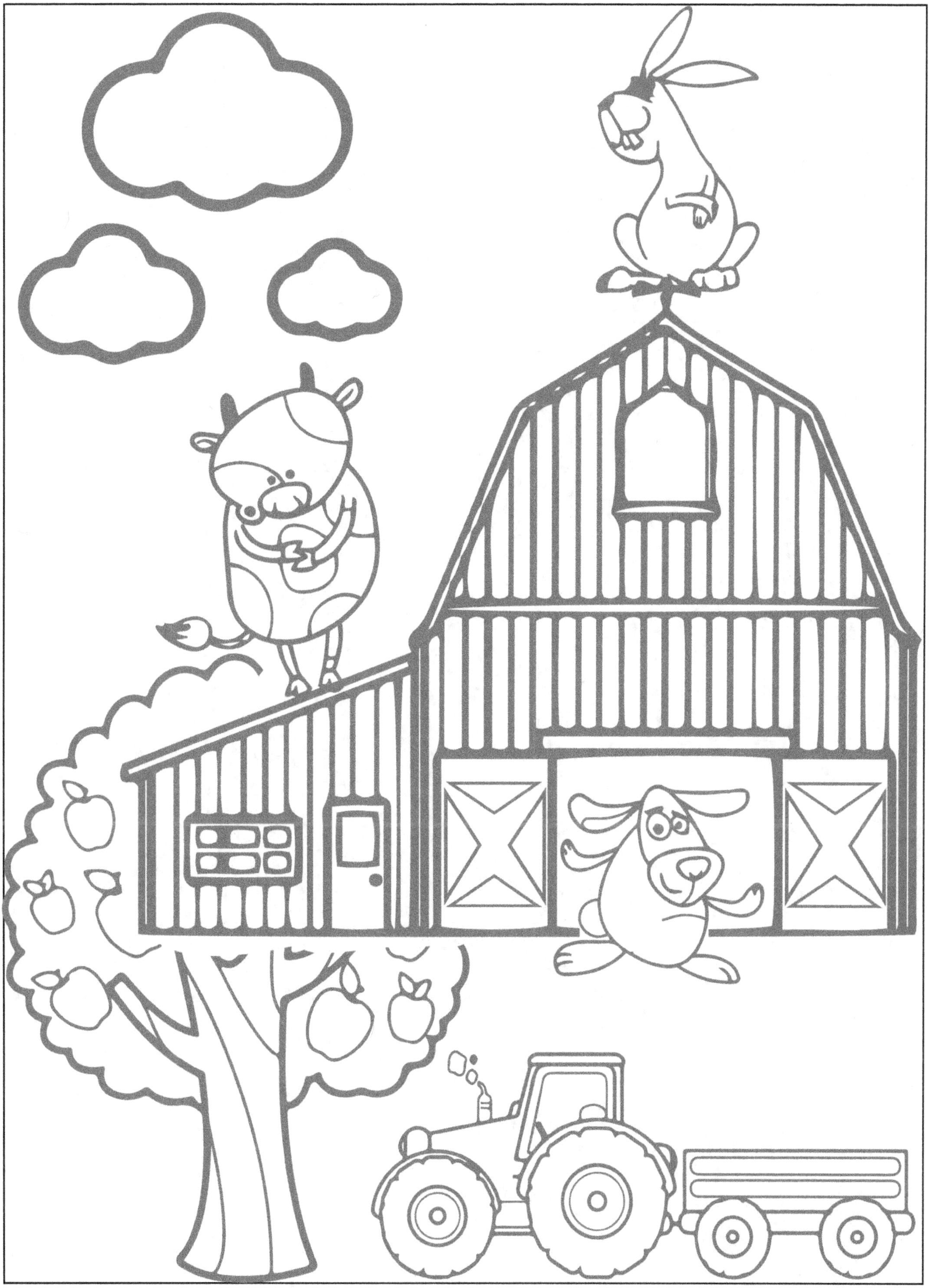

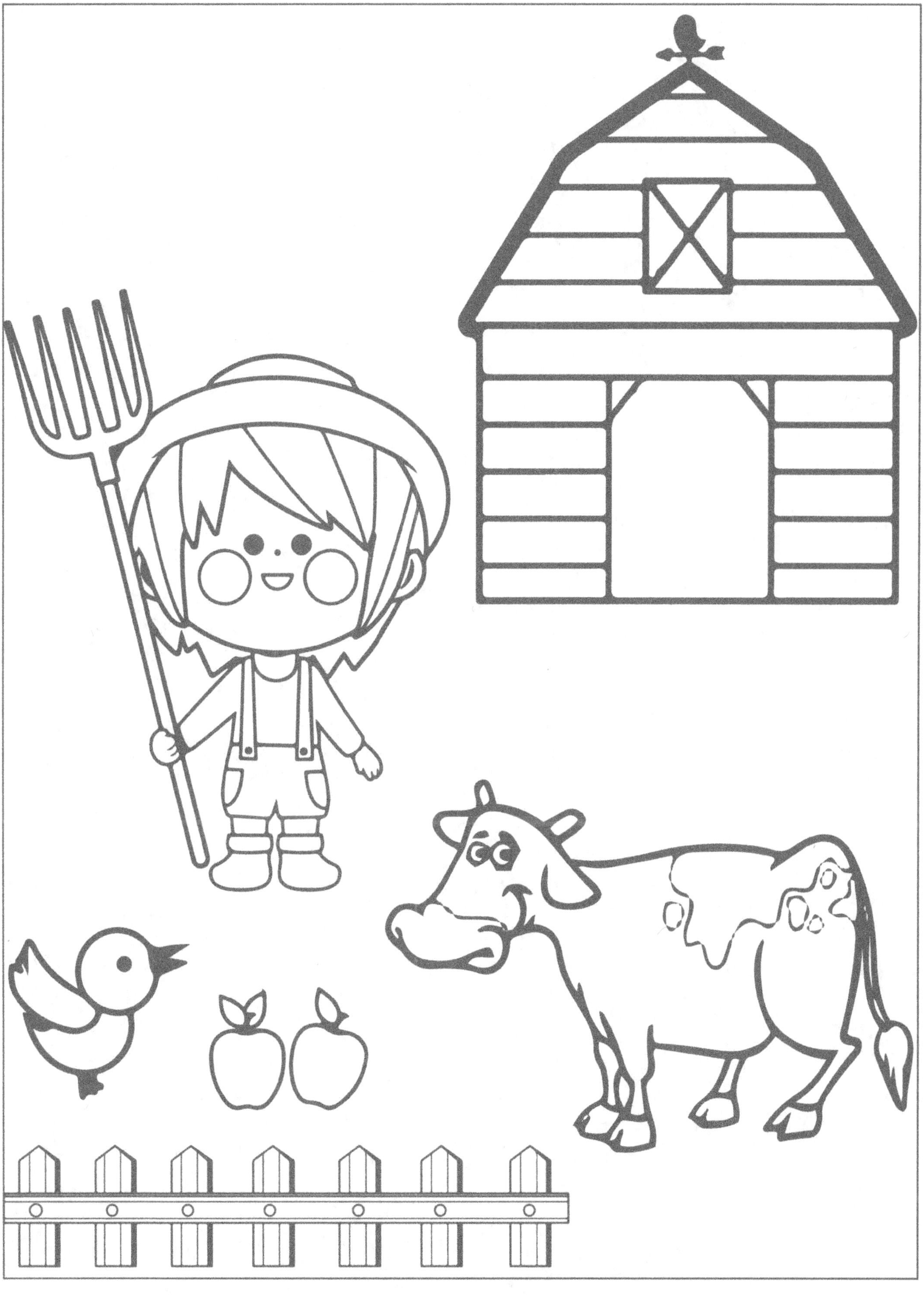

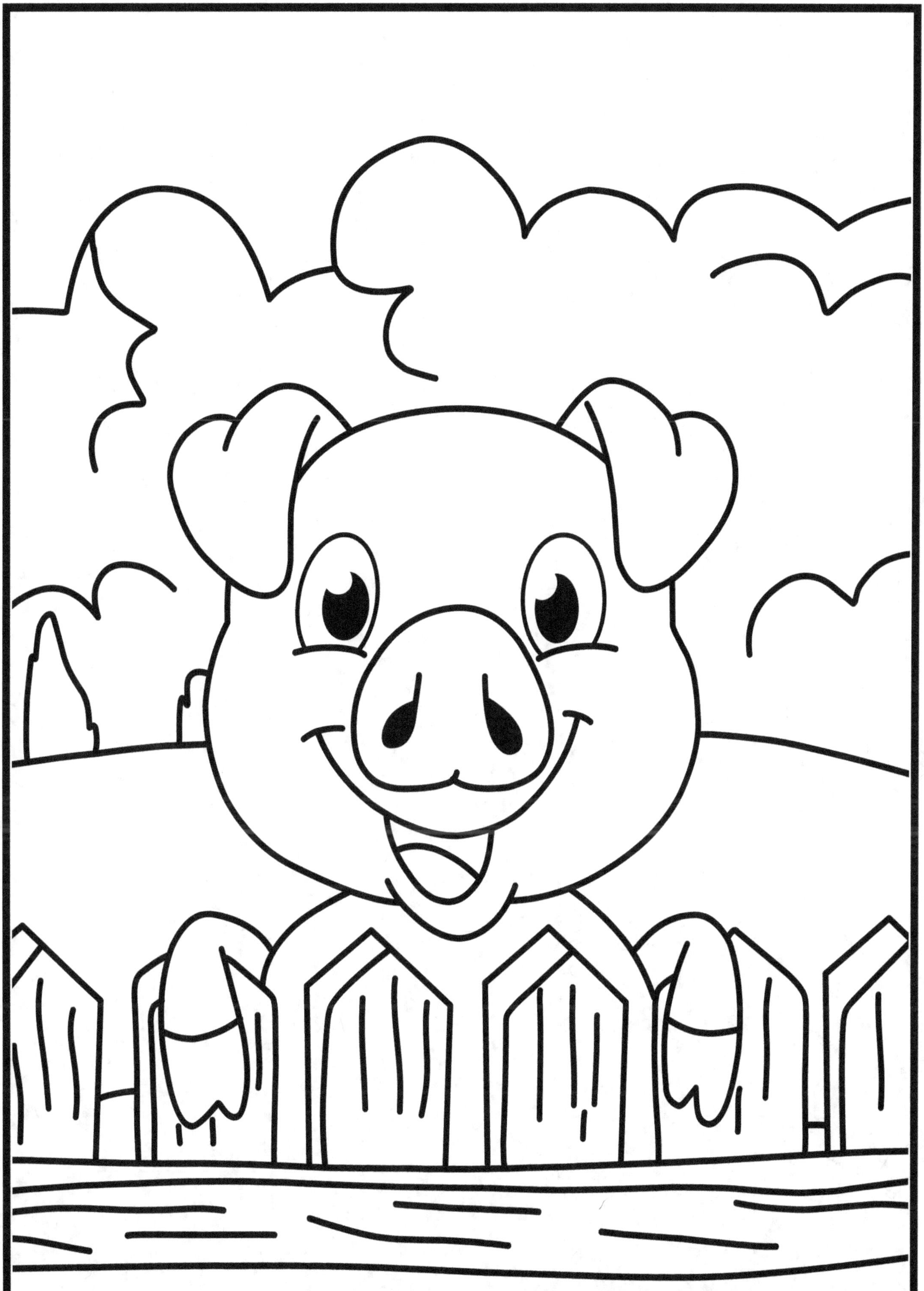

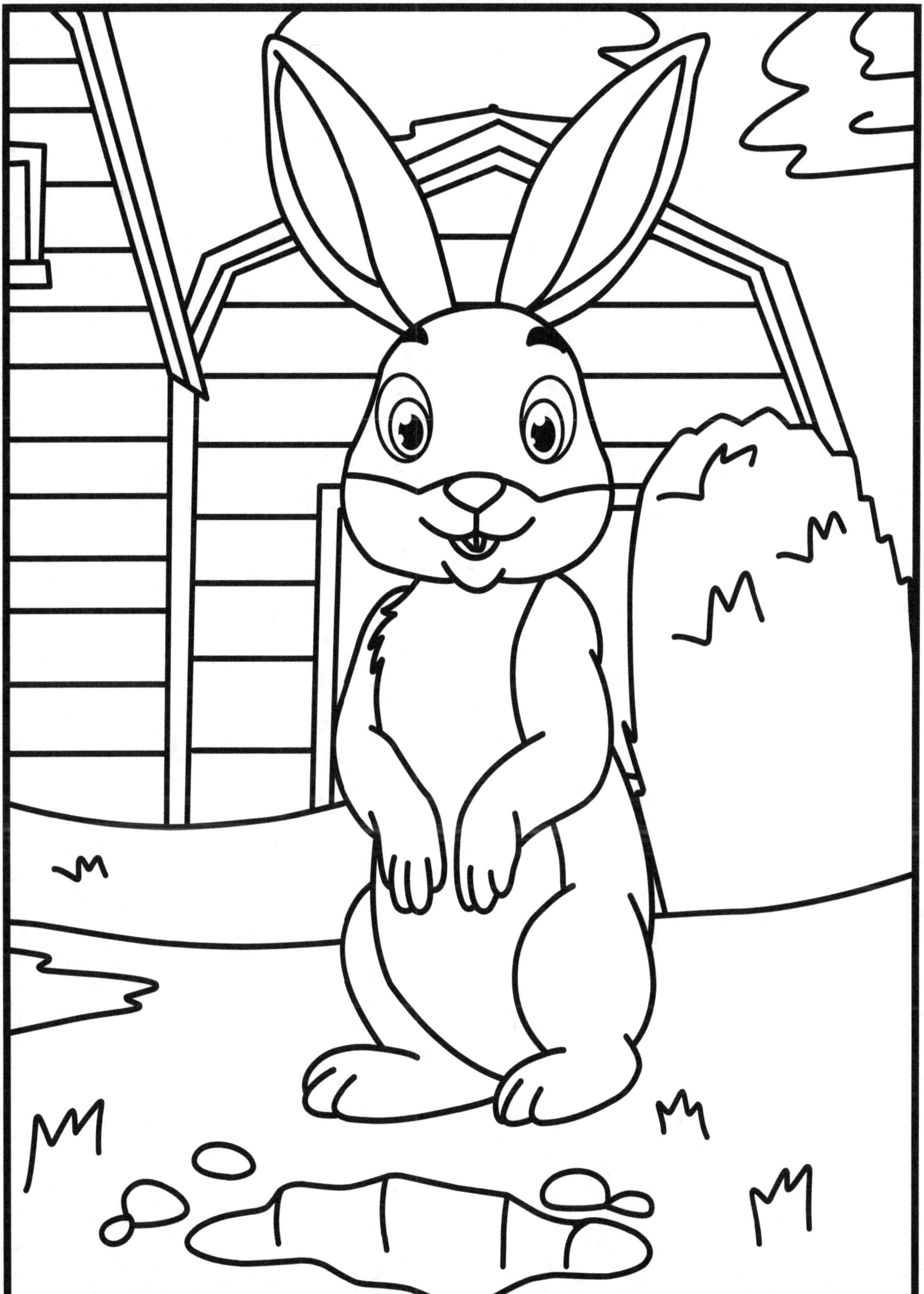

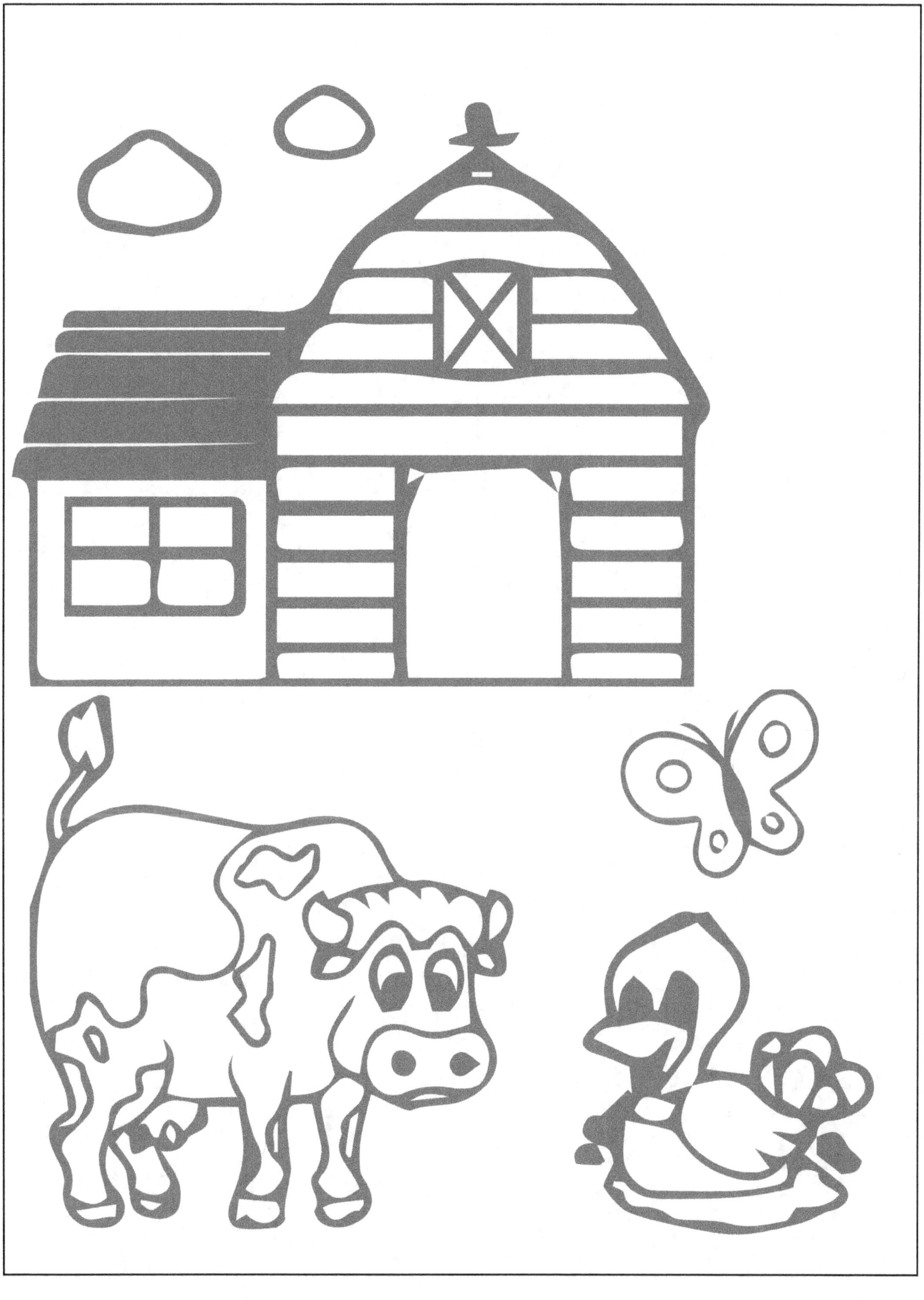

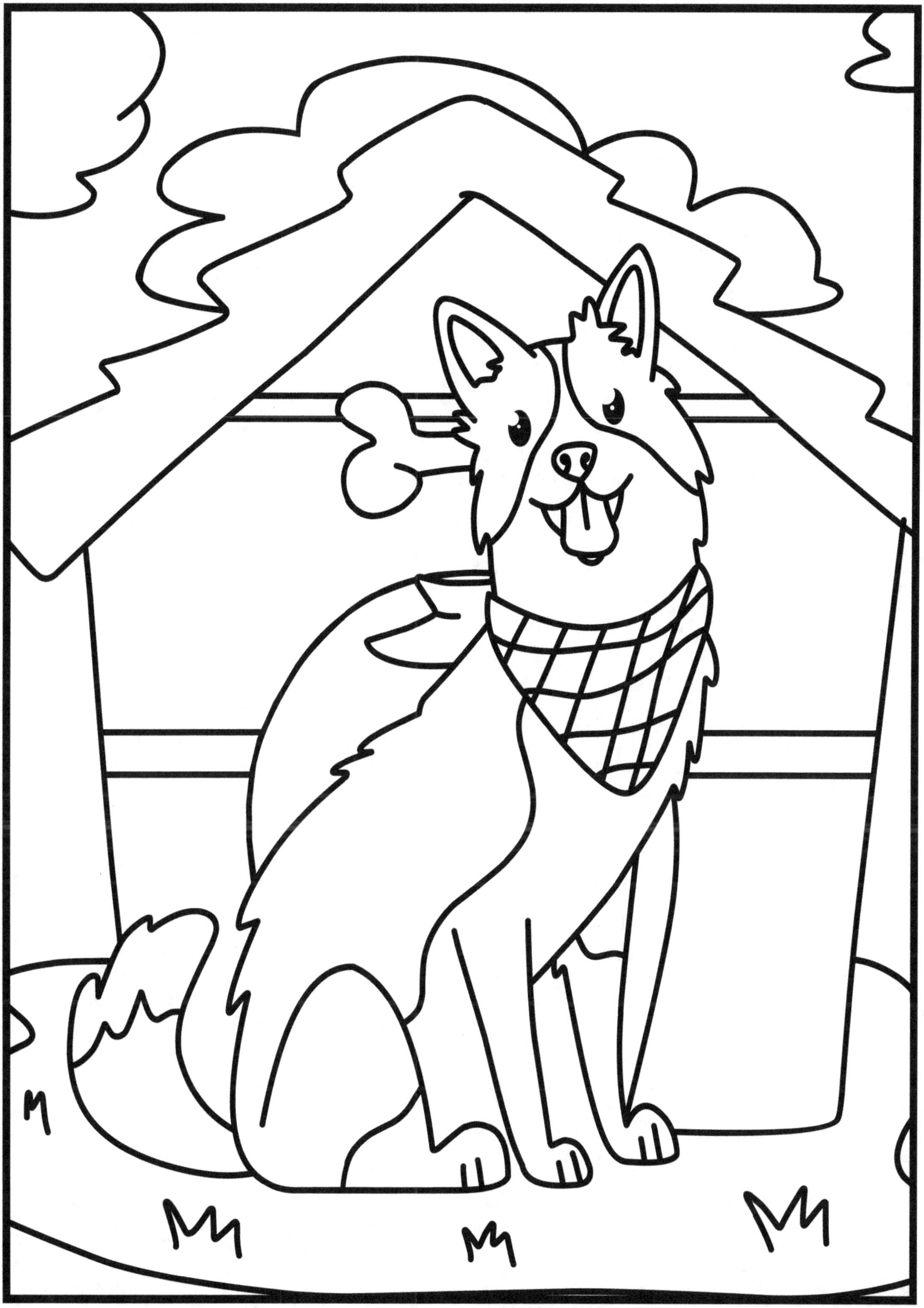

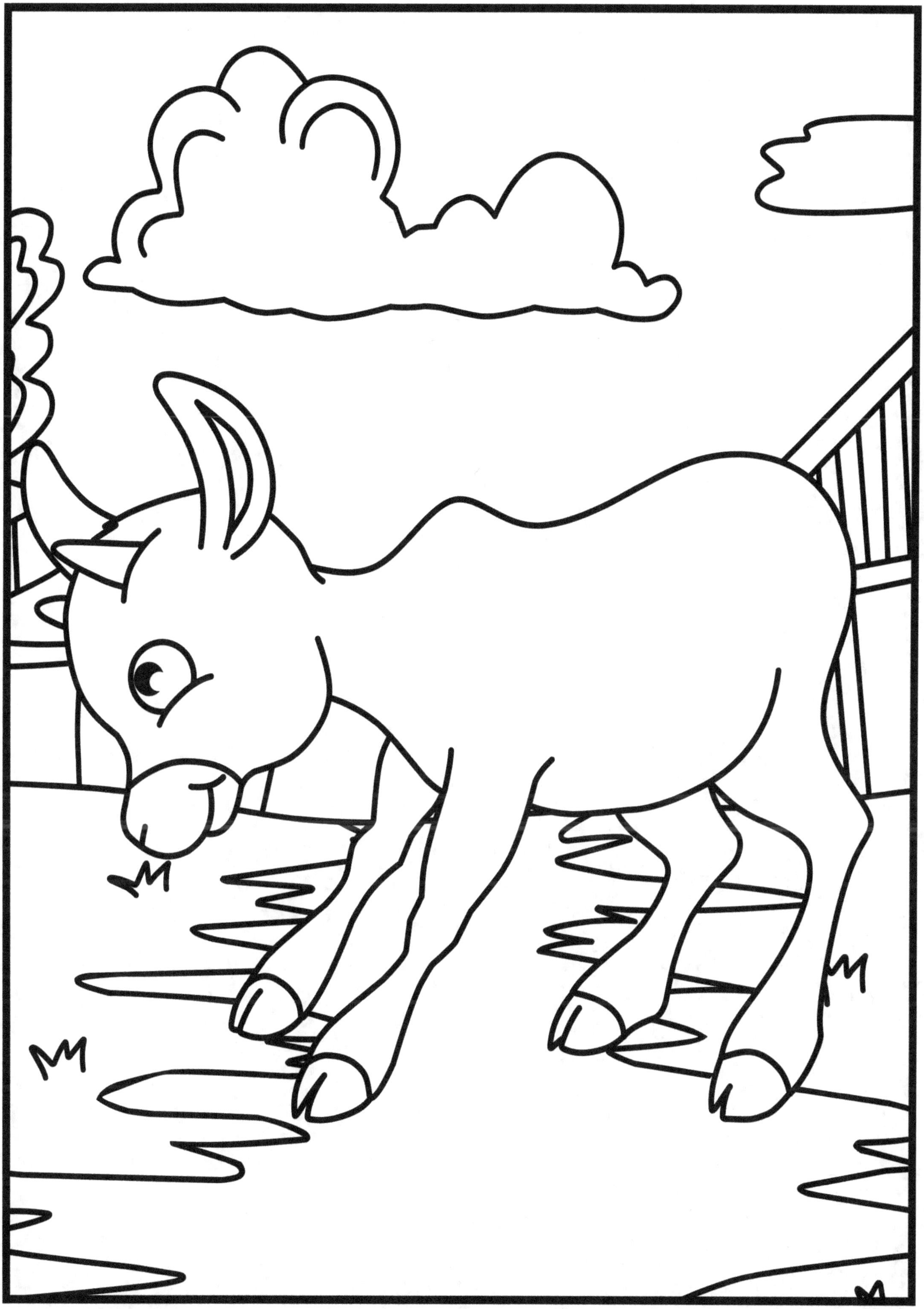

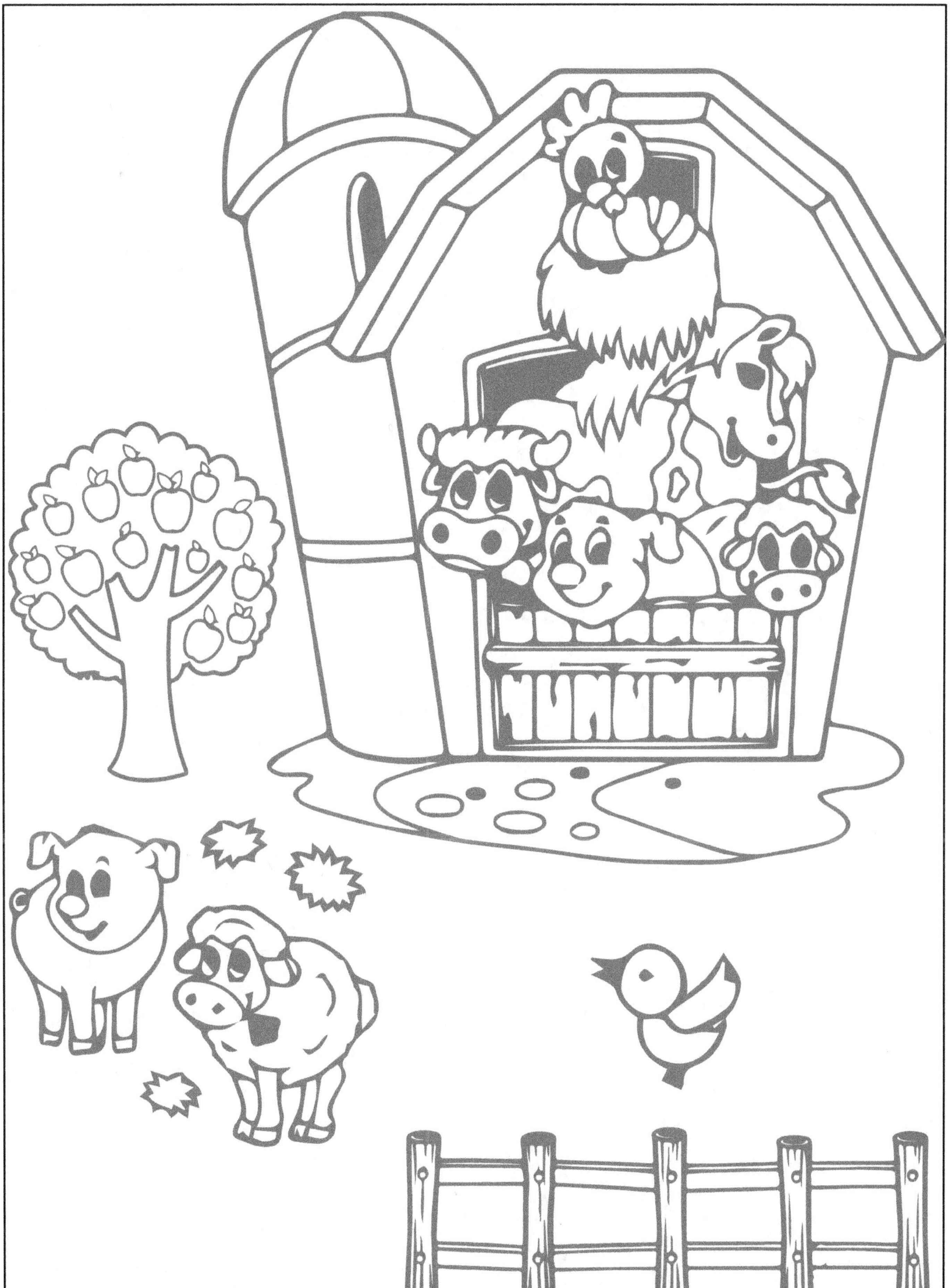

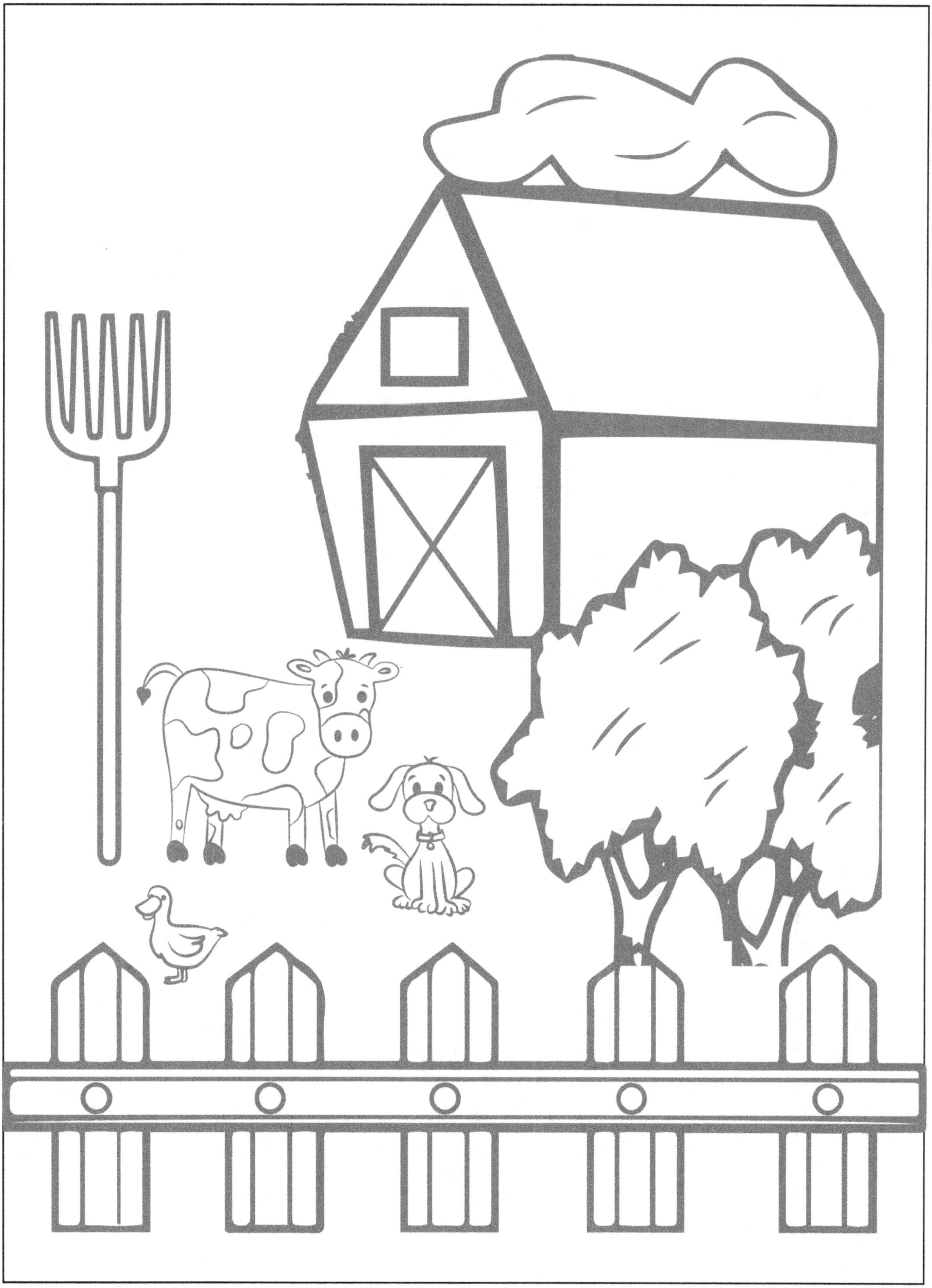

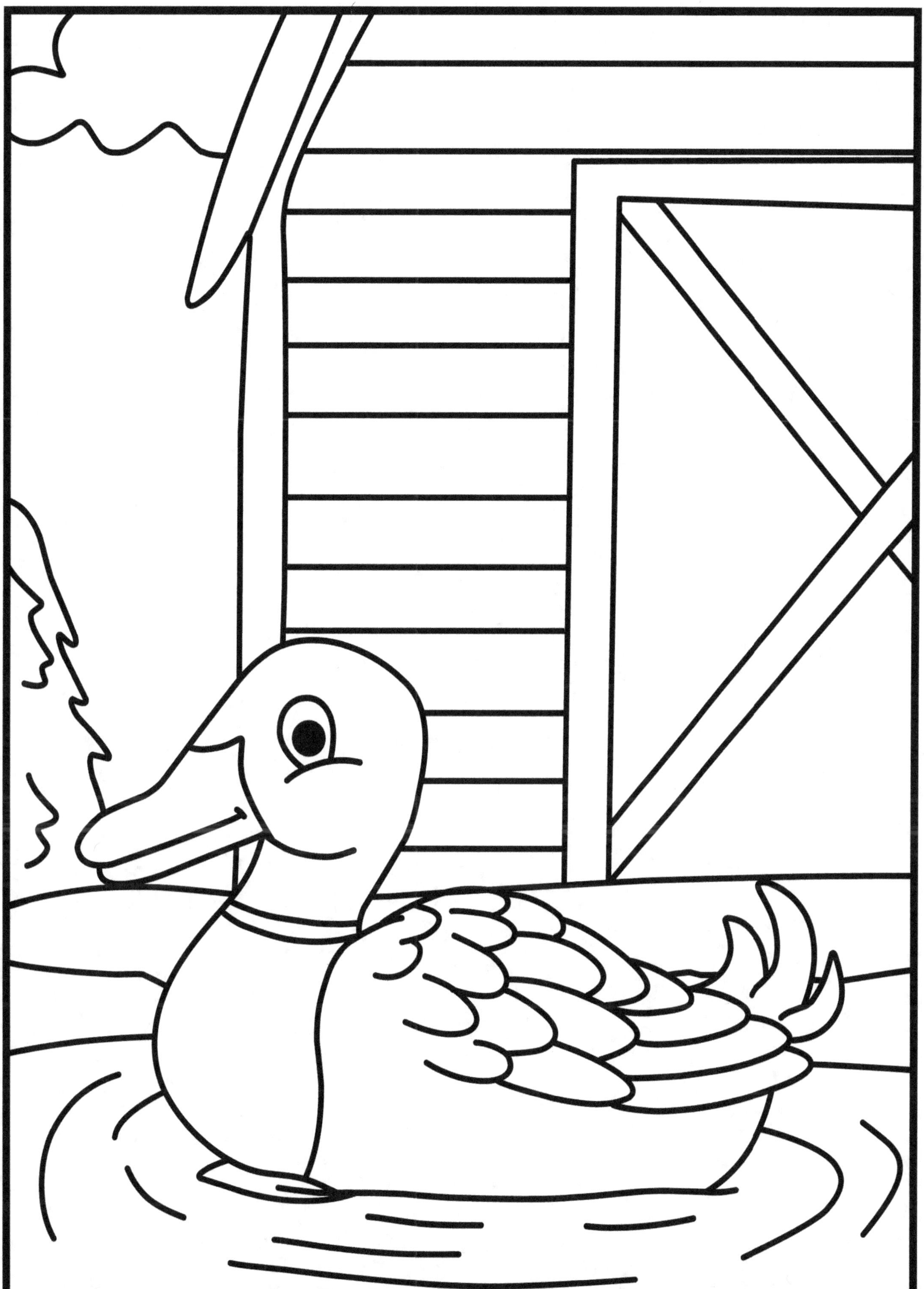

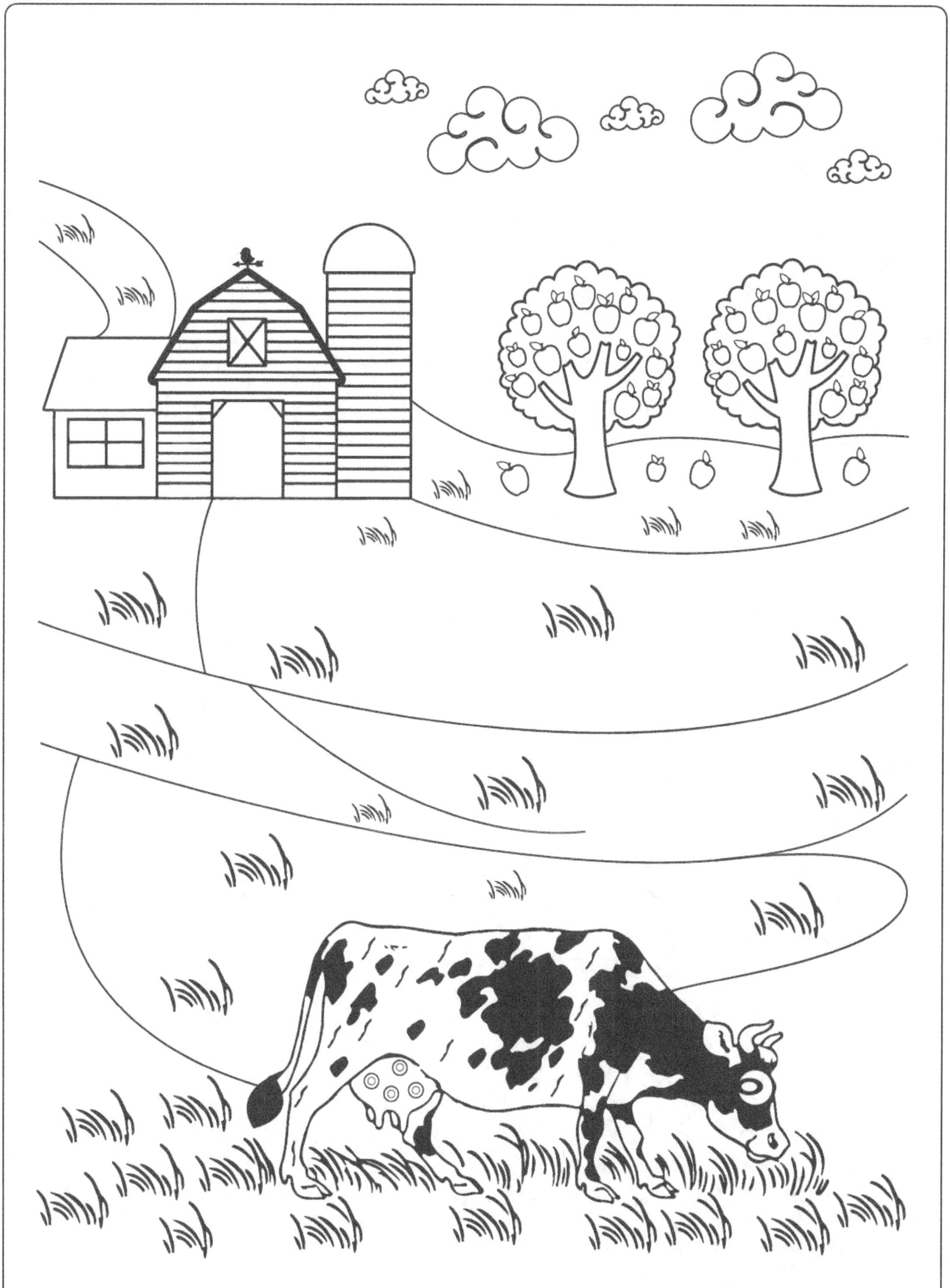

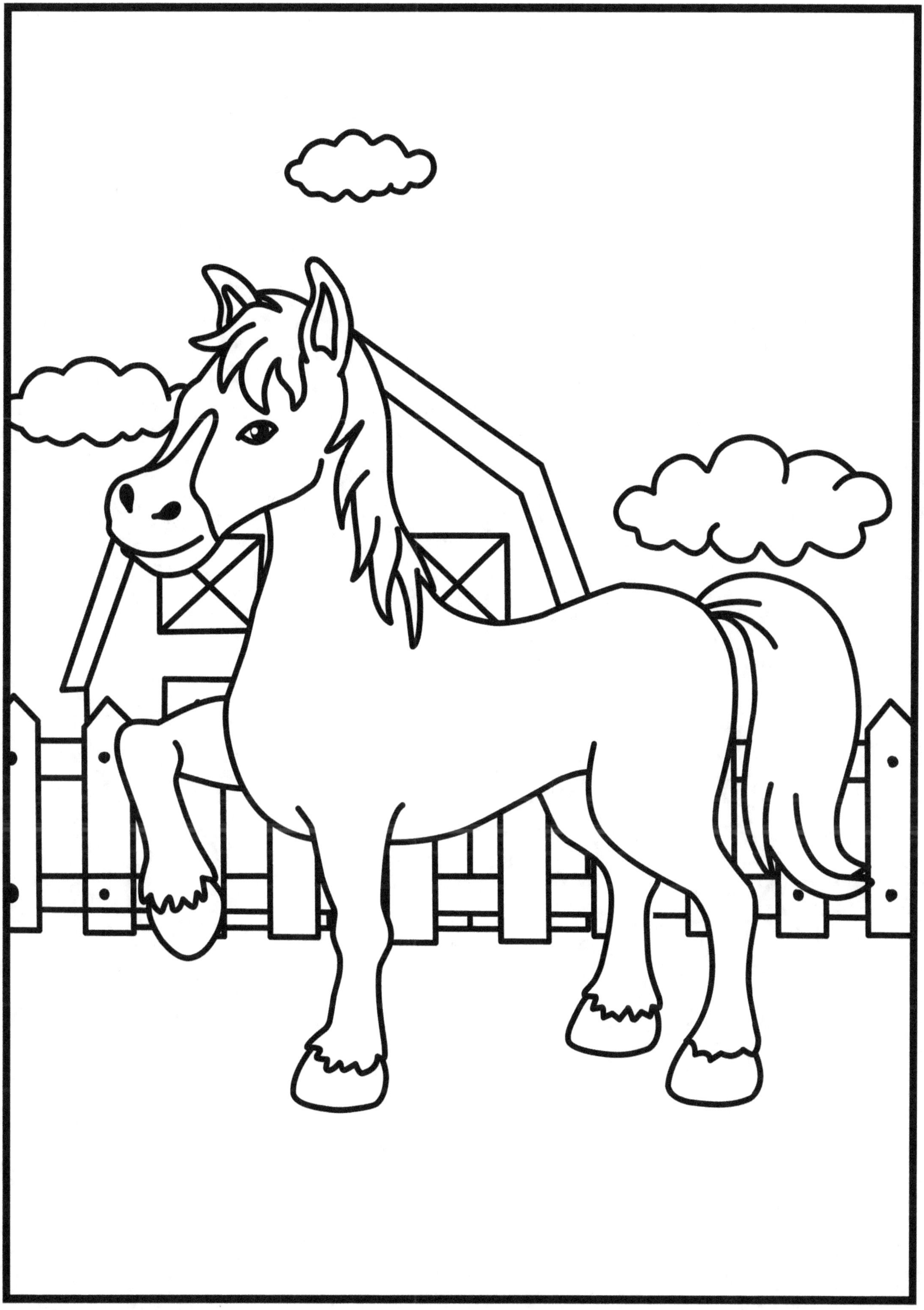

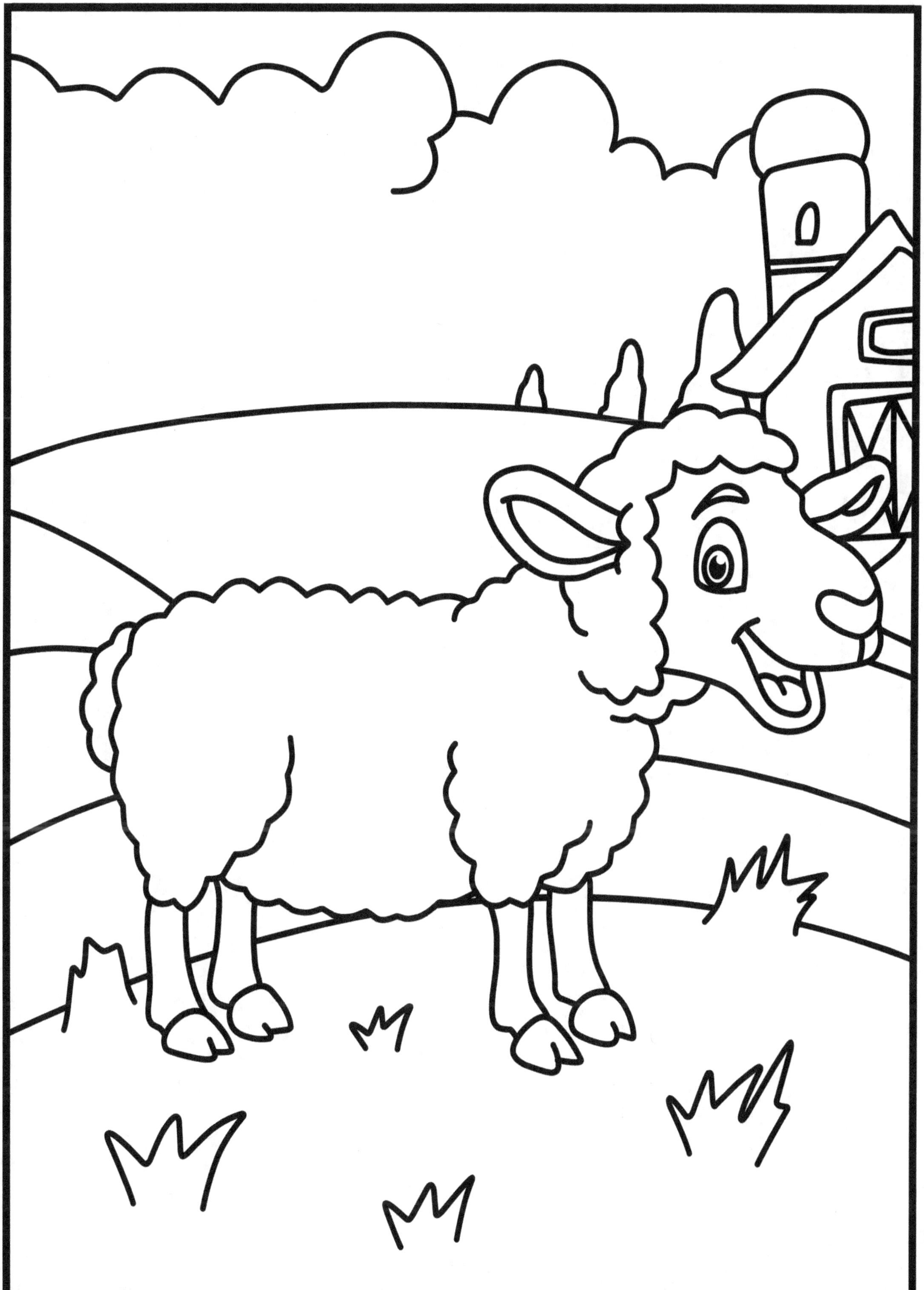

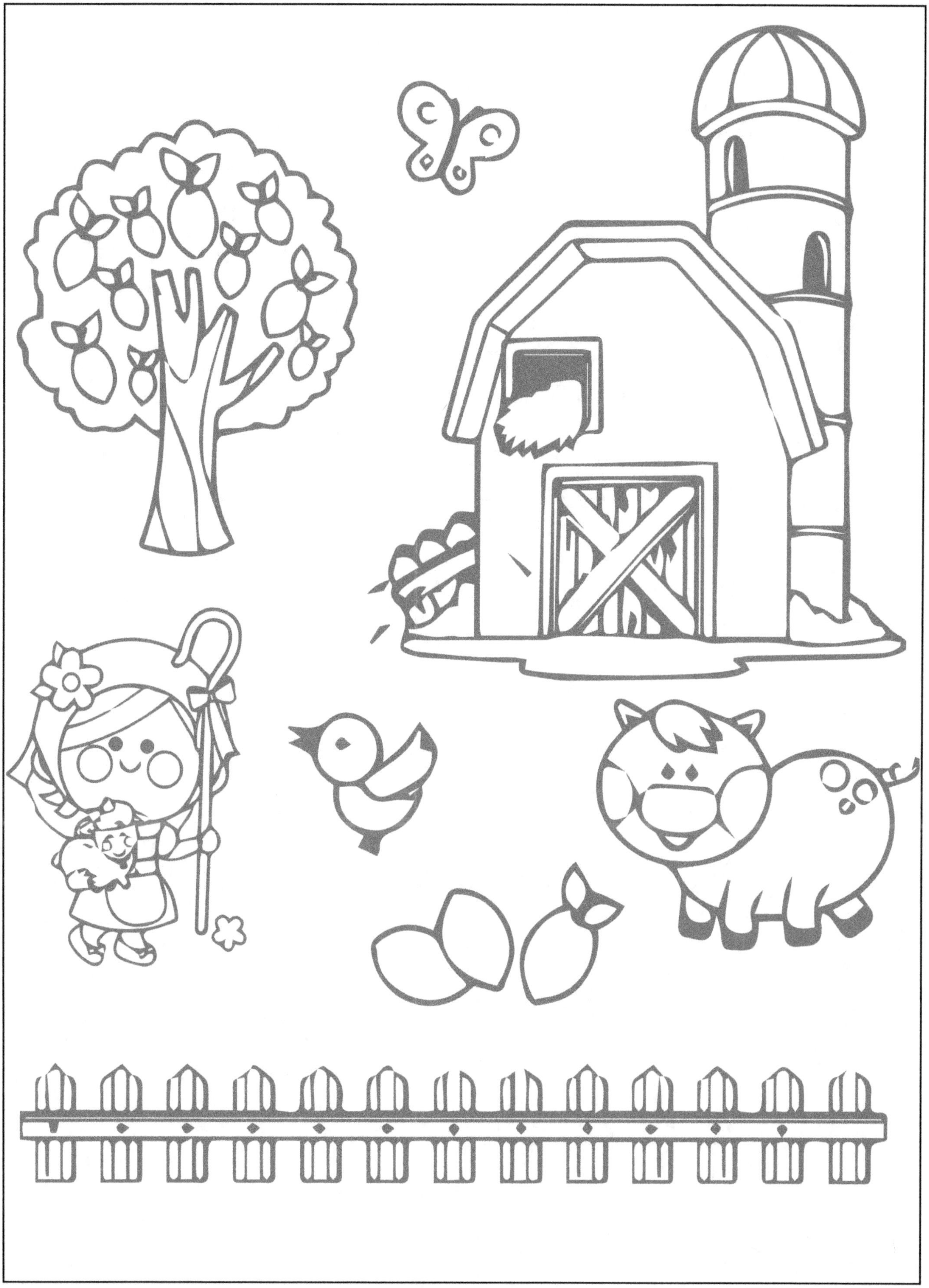

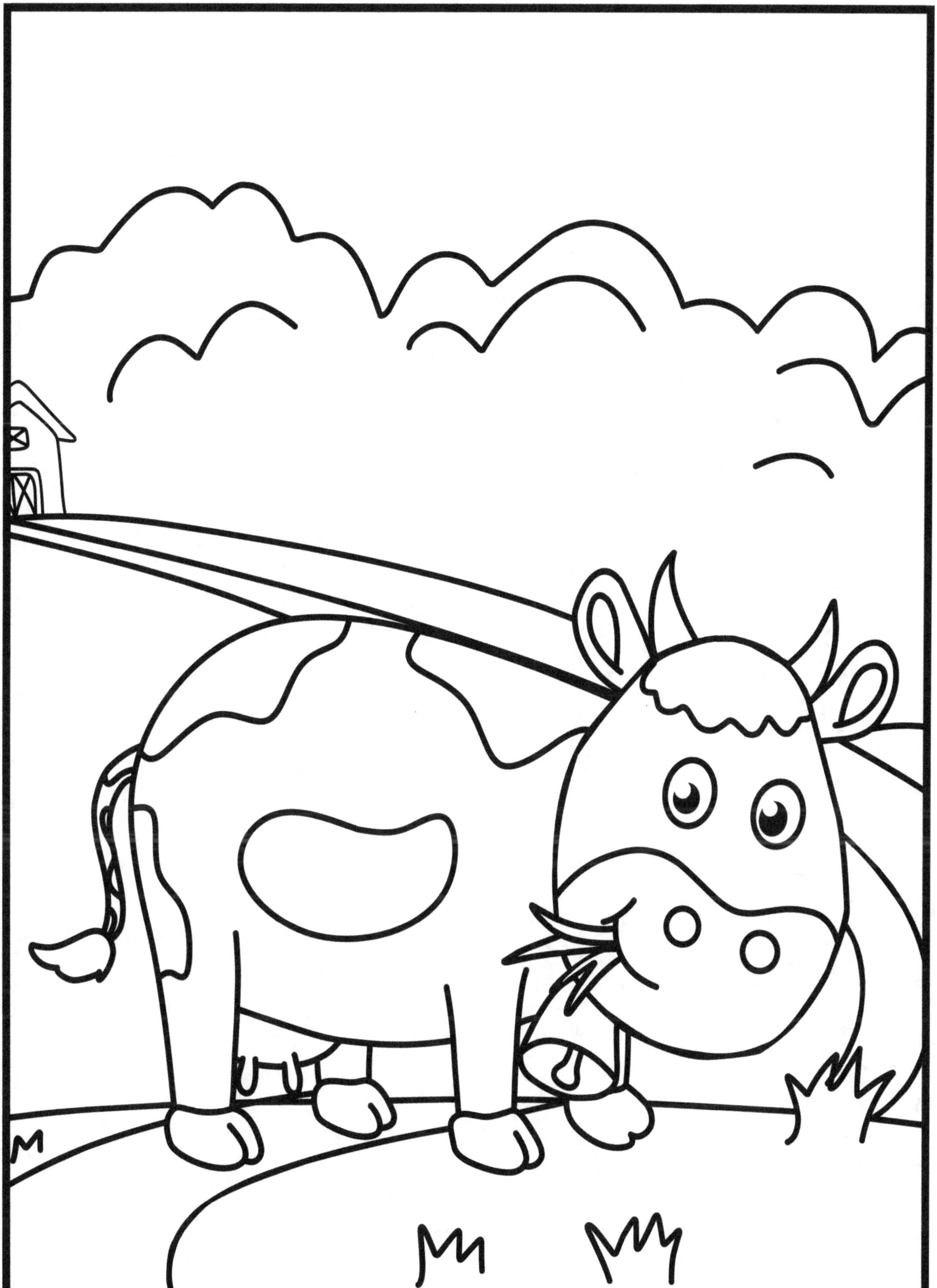

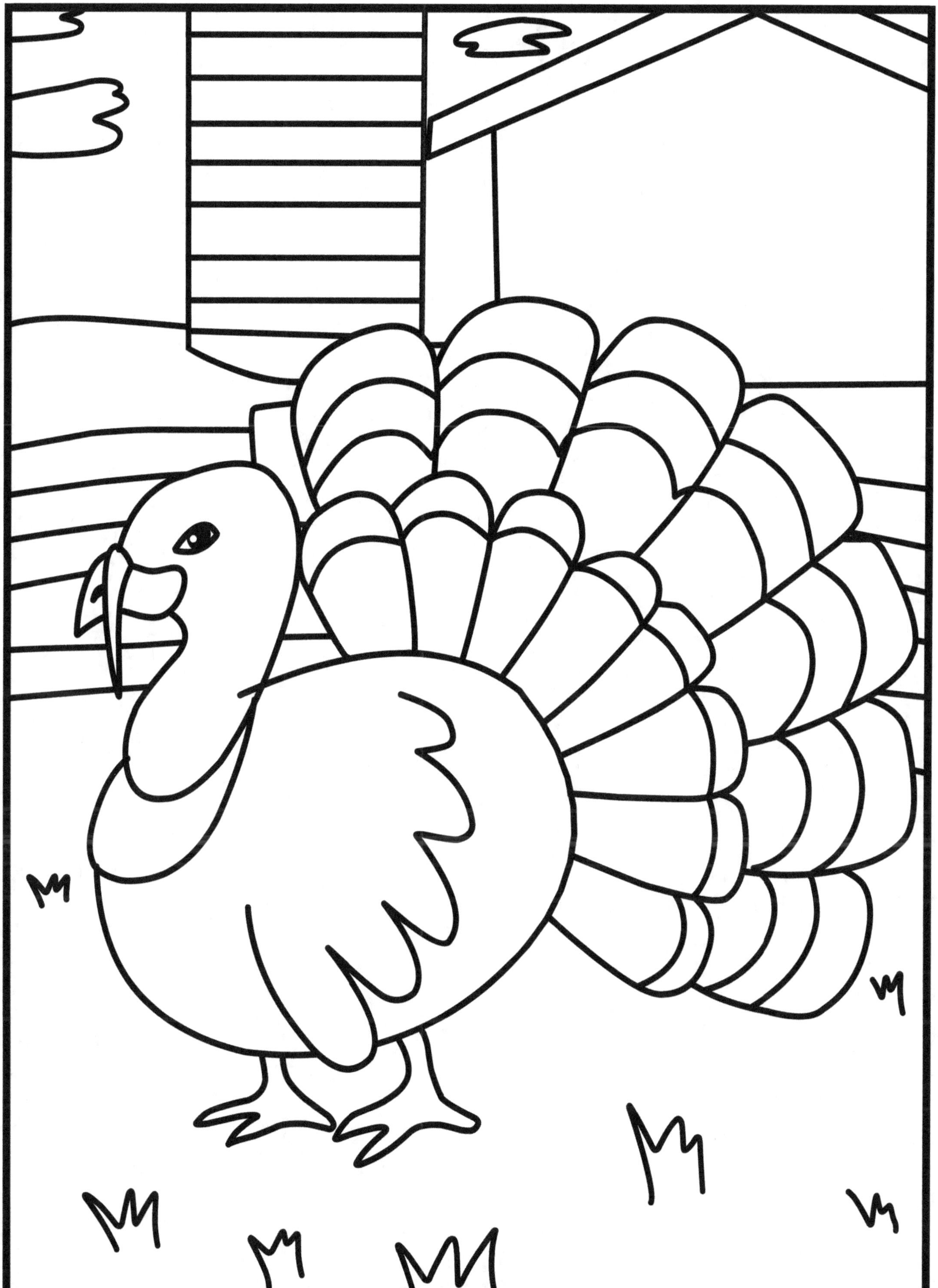

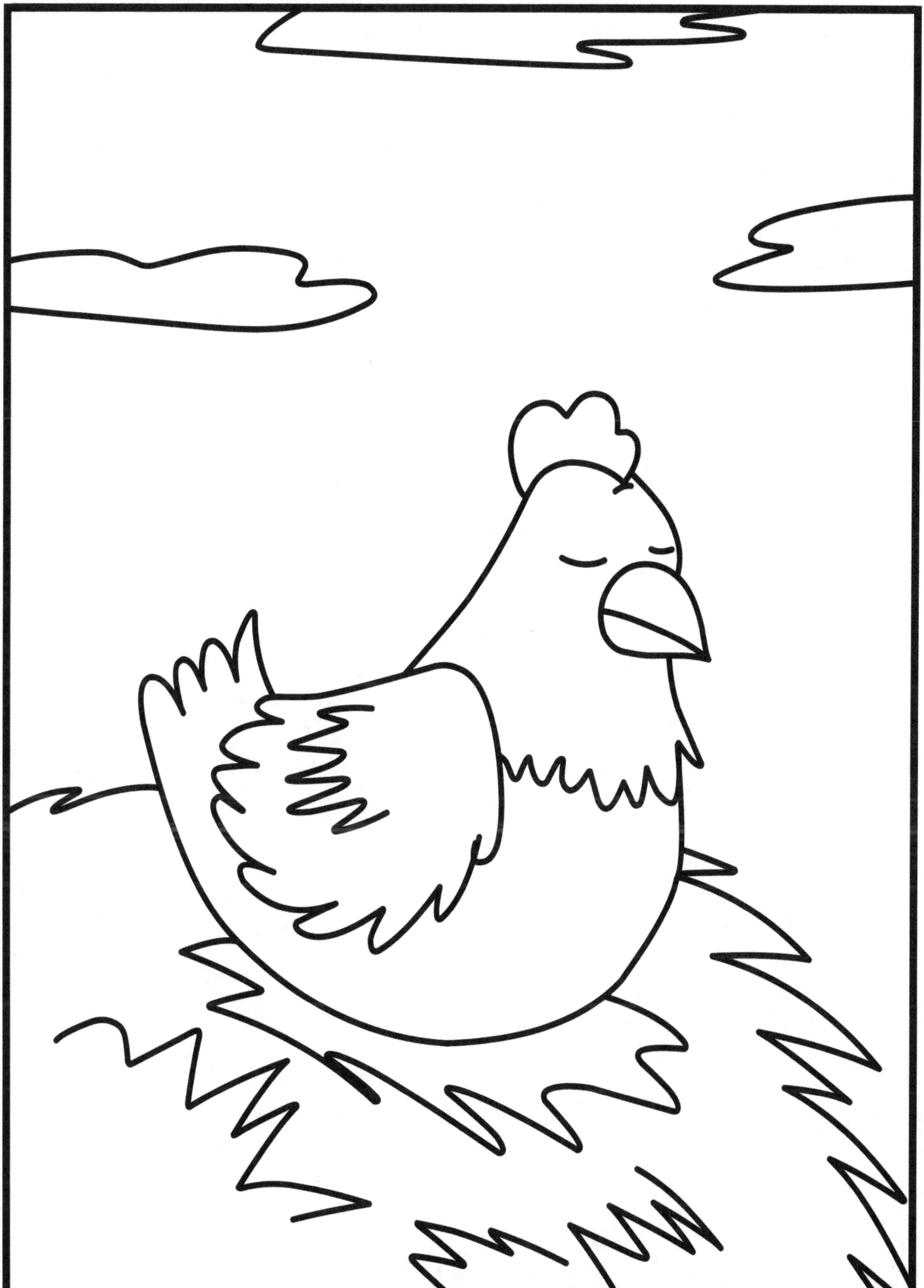

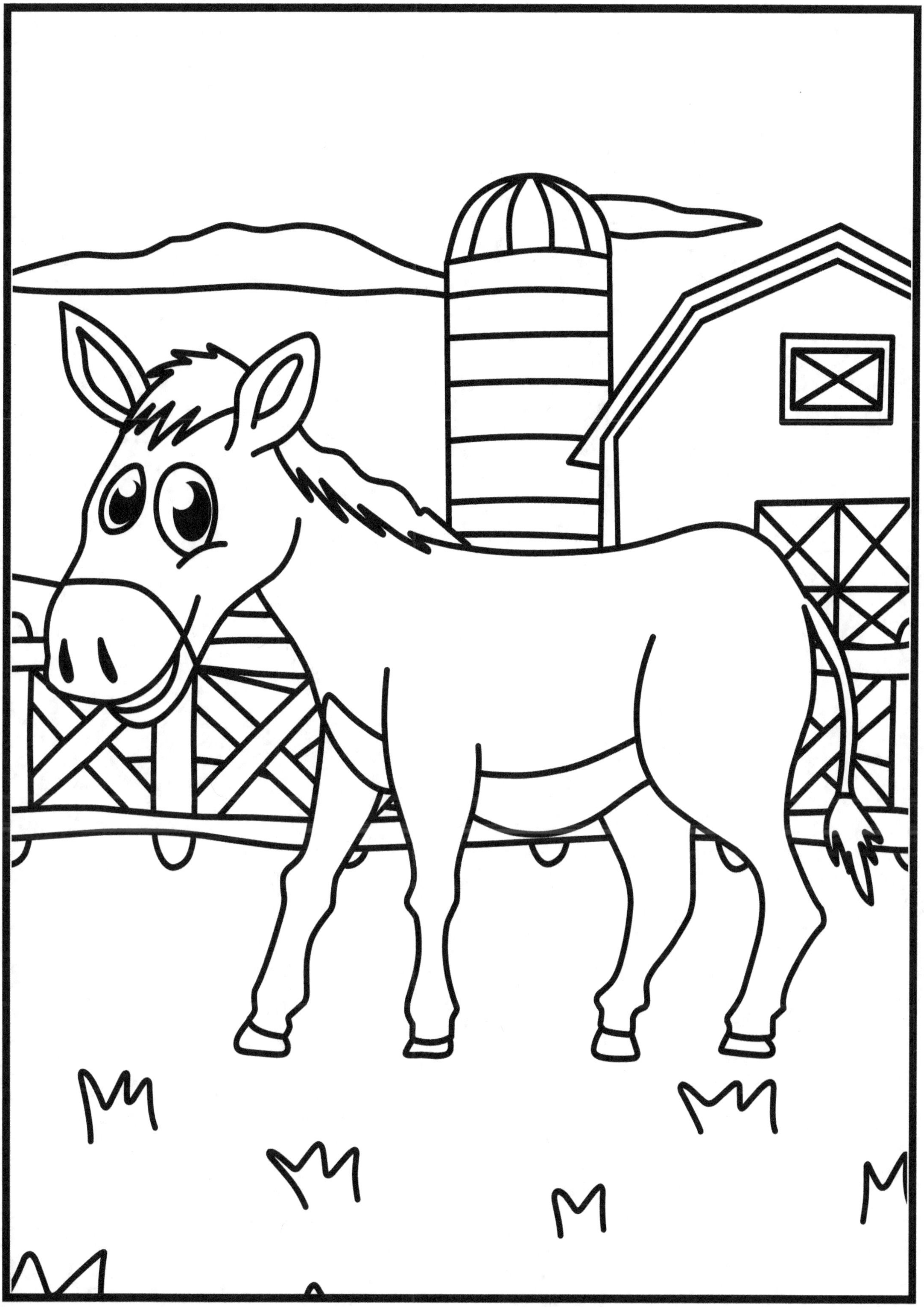

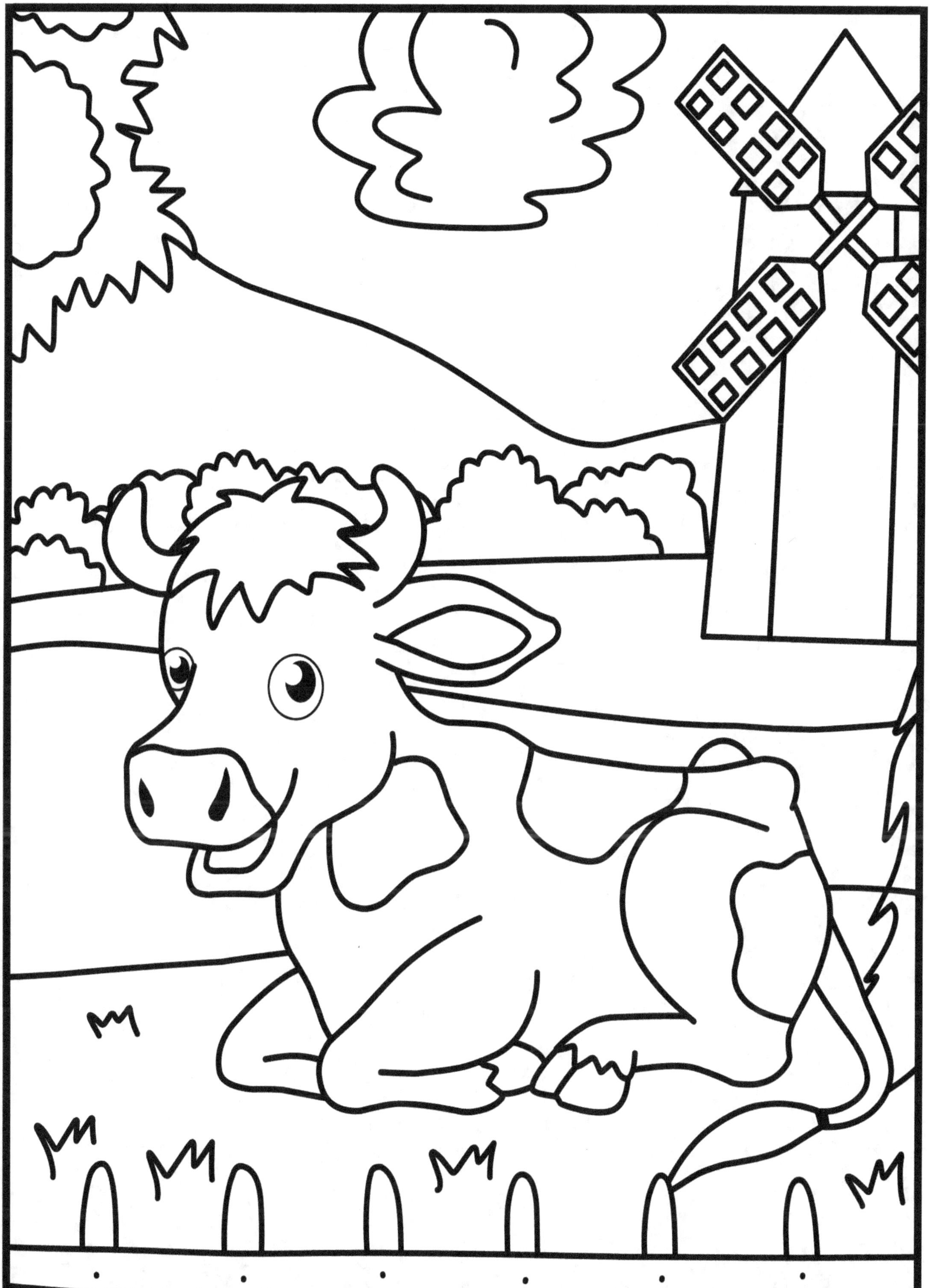

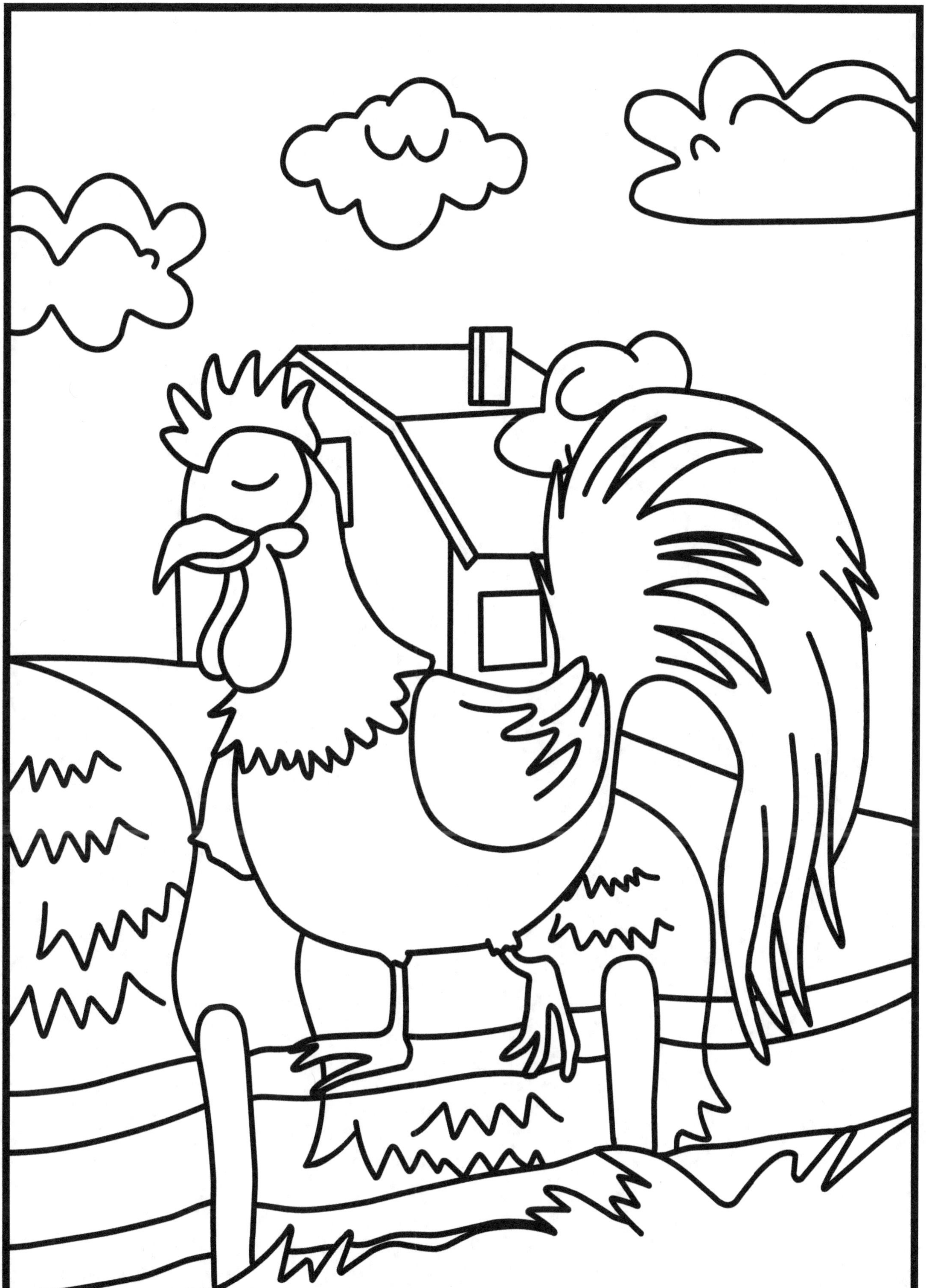

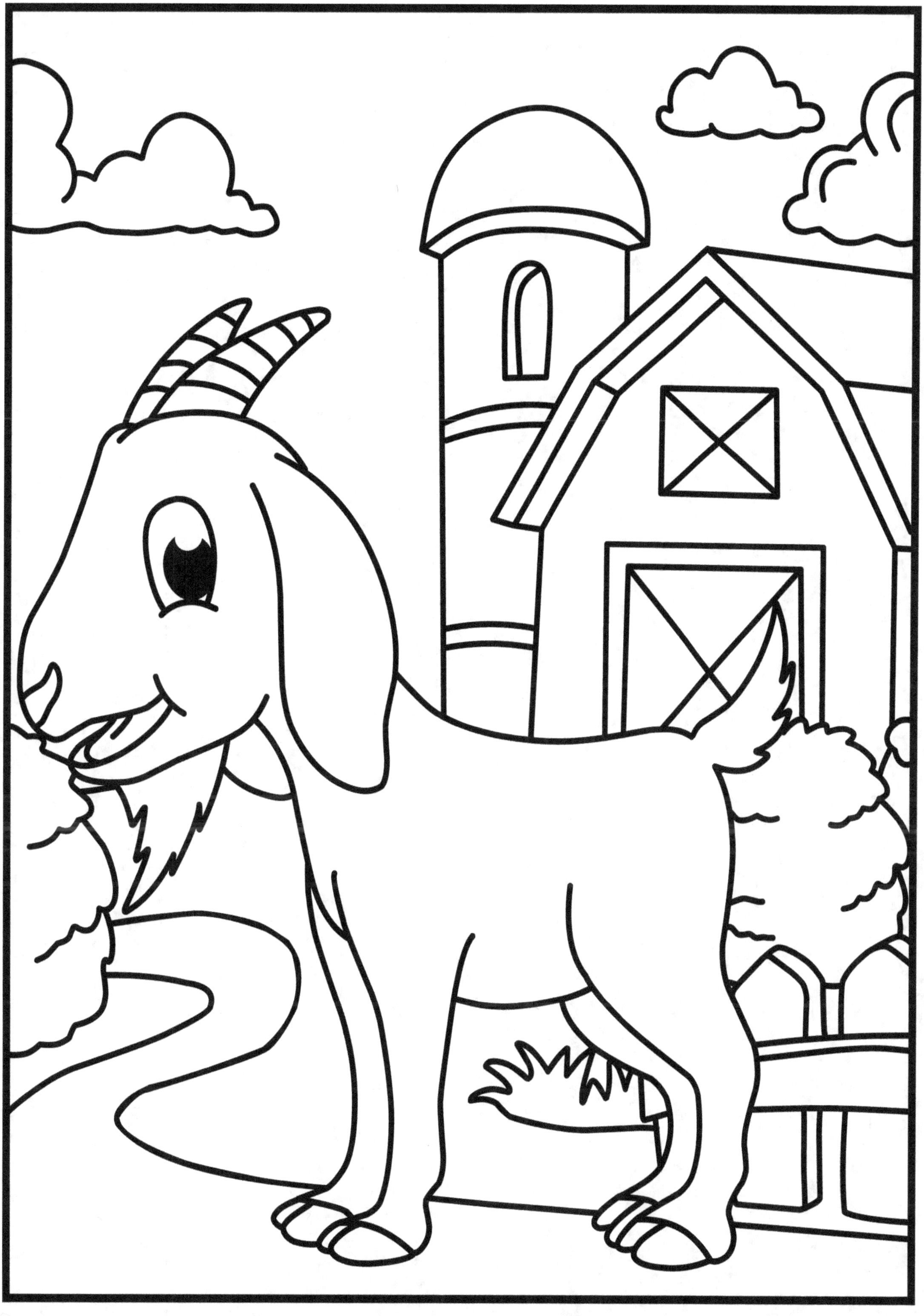

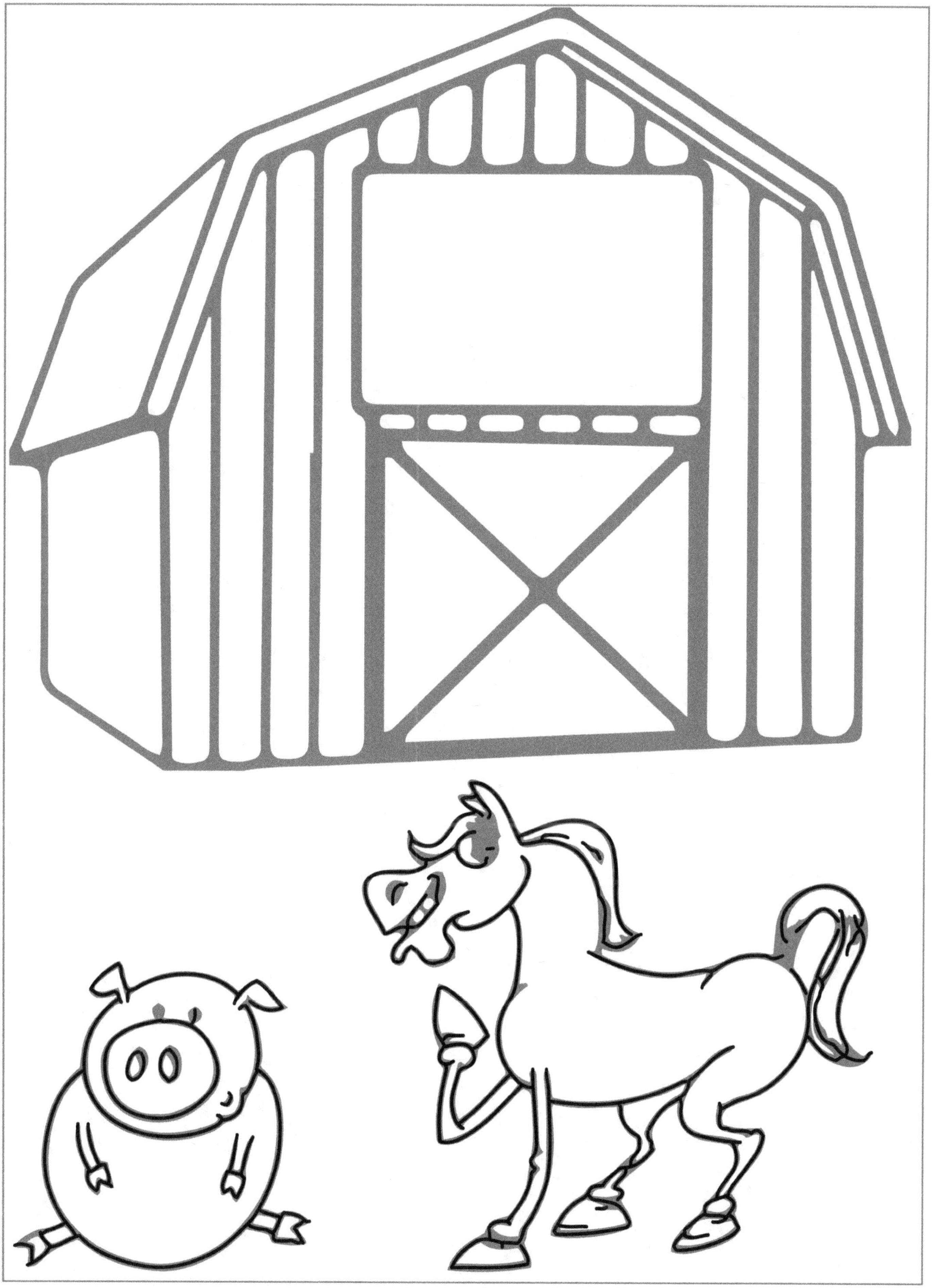

www.ingramcontent.com/pod-product-compliance
Lightning Source LLC
Chambersburg PA
CBHW082118220526
45472CB00009B/2231
* 9 7 9 8 4 5 4 2 2 5 1 8 6 *